Managers in the Middle

MANAGERS IN THE MIDDLE

A Harvard Business Review Paperback

Harvard Business Review paperback No. 90060

The *Harvard Business Review* articles in this collection
are available as individual reprints, with the exception of
"General Managers in the Middle." Discounts apply to
quantity purchases. For information and ordering contact
Operations Department, Harvard Business School Publishing
Division, Boston, MA 02163. Telephone: (617) 495-6192,
9 a.m. to 5 p.m. EST. Fax: (617) 495-6985, 24 hours a day.

Editor's Note: Some articles in this book may have been written before authors and editors began to take into consideration the role of women in management. We hope the archaic
usage representing all managers as male does not detract from
the usefulness of the collection.

Contents

Mastering
Middle Management

Hugo E.R. Uyterhoeven

General managers
in the middle

*A strong constitution and a juggler's finesse
are assets in what may well be the
major challenge of a rising manager's career*

Foreword

Having a boss's responsibility without a boss's authority; functioning as a specialist and a generalist at the same time; meeting the conflicting demands of superiors, subordinates, and peers while still getting the job done—these exacting requirements sound like part of a manager's nightmare. But, according to this author, they are daily facets of general management at middle levels of an organization, where risk and opportunity go hand in hand. While these general management positions are increasingly common in divisionalized corporations, they are often misunderstood by both middle managers and their superiors. In this article, the author discusses the demanding requirements of the job from a top-management and a middle-management perspective, and shows how it represents an opportunity for individual and corporate growth.

Mr. Uyterhoeven is Professor of Business Administration at the Harvard Business School and Faculty Chairman of the Advanced Management Program. He has been active in the areas of executive development, strategic planning, corporate organization, and international business.

Traditionally, the job of general manager has been equated with that of a company's chief executive. General manager and boss have been thought of synonymously. Yet, increasingly, corporate organizations are providing for general management positions at levels below the chief executive; and, as a result, the number of general managers at the middle level is rising.

The middle-level general manager phenomenon (i.e., a general manager who is responsible for a particular business unit at the intermediate level of the corporate hierarchy) is a direct outgrowth of the movement toward a divisional form of organization. For example, while the *functional* organization requires only one general manager, the *divisional* organization provides for a variety of business units, each requiring a general manager. Often the process of divisionalization extends several levels down into the organization (i.e., group, division, department), further increasing the need for general managers at lower levels.

The shift from functional to divisional organization occurred in the United States largely during the last two decades and is currently taking place in Europe. It is a worldwide phenomenon necessitated by the greater product-line diversity as well as the growing international operations of a vast majority of the larger corporations.

Although the divisional organization is now a familiar phenomenon, little attention has been directed at obtaining a clear understanding of the middle-level general management position. Of course, one approach would be to refer to what is known about the top-level general manager, but this knowledge is not really applicable —the two positions are significantly different. Furthermore, general management at the middle organizational level is, in a number of respects, more difficult.

In this article, I shall attempt to (a) define the characteristics and responsibilities of the middle-level general manager's job and (b) draw the implications for the individual assigned to it (hereafter referred to as "middle manager") as well as for the company that employs him.

Managing relationships

The middle manager, like most managers, accomplishes his goals largely by managing relationships. There are few things which a manager

ing the middle manager to act as subordinate, equal, and superior:

○ Upward, he relates to his boss as a subordinate; he takes orders.

○ Downward, he relates to his team as a superior; he gives orders.

○ Laterally, he often relates to peers in the organization as an equal; for example, he may have to secure cooperation from a pooled sales force or solicit assistance from corporate staff services.

Thus the middle manager wears three hats in fulfilling his general management role. In contrast, the top-level general manager acts primarily as a superior—this alone is a significant difference between the two positions.

Managing the triple set of relationships is most demanding; it is analogous to a baseball player having to excel simultaneously in hitting, fielding, and pitching. The middle manager must be able not only to manage all three relationships,

but also to shift quickly and frequently from one to another.

In view of these conflicting and changing demands, it is often difficult for the middle manager to arrive at a consistent pattern of behavior. Moreover, in the process of satisfying the re-

can do alone; he must usually rely on the support, cooperation, or approval of a large number of people. As the textbooks say, he "gets things done through others."

Managing relationships at his level in the organization, however, is a threefold task, requir-

quirements of one set of relationships he may reduce his effectiveness in managing another. For instance, a middle manager who follows orders from headquarters to the letter may thereby, in the eyes of subordinates, either weaken his authority or appear unreasonable and unresponsive. Consider this illustration from an internationally divisionalized company:

Headquarters restricted the freedom of one division manager to purchase from the outside, an order which threatened to undermine his authority as a general manager. He was torn between the dilemma of (a) asserting his authority with his subordinates by ignoring or fighting headquarters' orders, or (b) weakening his image as a superior by following headquarters' orders. Being a good subordinate would have weakened him as a superior; yet, by being a strong superior, he would have been a disloyal subordinate. As it turned out, the general manager held prolonged negotiations with a peer in the pooled sales force to arrive at a mutually satisfactory solution, but this made the general manager appear inconclusive and indecisive to his subordinates.

In order to successfully manage such multiple relationships, and their often conflicting and changing demands, the middle manager should recognize the full scope of his job. For instance, he should:

1. Make the network of relationships explicit. To whom does he have to relate? What are the key relationships?

2. Identify, in his specific situation, the triple set of requirements. What is expected of him as a good subordinate? What is required to be an effective colleague and equal? And what does it take to provide leadership as a superior? This analysis should force the middle manager to focus not only on his own goals and abilities but also on those of his "opposite numbers" at all three levels.

3. Recognize the difficulty of achieving consistent behavior in view of conflicting demands and be willing to wear three hats at the same time. Success will involve the balancing of all three roles. Sometimes it requires trade-offs. Under such complex circumstances, it helps to proceed explicitly.

4. Communicate his understanding of the job to others in the organization with whom he must relate. (These others should bear in mind that, singly, they are part of but one of the multiple relationship sets that he has to manage; their expectations and responses should take this into account.)

A playing coach

In some respects, the middle manager is the leader of his unit who delegates, guides, and plans; in other respects, however, he has specific operating responsibilities and must "roll up his sleeves" to achieve output and to meet his targets. Therefore, he is both a delegator and a doer, both a strategist and an operator, or, to use another sports analogy, both a coach and a player. In contrast, his superiors are usually coaches and his subordinates are normally players.

Continuing the analogy, sports experience indicates that it is easier to excel either as a coach or as a player and that the playing-coach job is clearly the most difficult—the skills of a successful player are different from those of a successful coach, but the playing coach must possess the skills of both. Likewise, the dual role of a middle manager combines different skills and actions. On the one hand, he needs a broad overview, detachment, and a long-run perspective. On the other hand, he needs detailed knowledge and experience, the ability to involve himself directly and deeply, and a sense of urgency.

Acting both as player and as coach, the middle manager must constantly balance the two roles and sometimes make trade-offs. Is he going to be too much of a player, too involved in operating details and in doing things himself? Or is he becoming too much of a coach by staying aloof, by delegating too much, by not getting sufficiently involved? It is easy to misperceive one's role, especially in regard to the latter. For example:

Top management in a large divisionalized corporation assigned a promising middle manager to a recent acquisition. Charged with enthusiasm for his new position, the manager saw himself as primarily a delegator, an organization builder whose job was to oversee the installation of parent company procedures and guide the acquisition's integration with staff services of the parent. He had not considered becoming directly involved in operating details or concentrating attention on increasing sales, both of which his immediate superior, the former owner/manager, saw as primary responsibilities of the middle-management position.

This question of balance—of asking oneself, "To what extent do I get involved in actual operations and to what extent do I delegate?"—is most delicate. And the balancing of the two roles is, of course, also influenced by the demands, expectations, and abilities of the middle manager's superiors and subordinates. The choice is not entirely free.

The bilingual manager

In keeping with his dual role, the middle manager usually receives abstract guidance from his superiors in the form of goals that he must translate into concrete action.

If, for example, a company's chief executive sets the goal of a certain percentage increase in earnings per share (and mentions it to financial analysts, thereby making it an even stronger commitment), how does he go about achieving this goal? He will communicate it to his group vice president, who will salute and pass it on to his divisional general manager, who, in turn, will salute and pass it on to the middle manager. The latter will salute, turn around, and find nobody to pass the goal on to. To use Harry Truman's famous dictum, this is where the buck stops.

The buck stops at the middle manager, who must assume the bilingual role of translating the strategic language of his superiors into the operational language of his subordinates in order to get results. He must turn the abstract guidance of, say, more earnings per share or meeting the budget into the concrete action required to achieve the results.

Often the middle manager is presented these abstract goals carrying the label, "difficult but achievable." While such labels may have a motivating purpose, they are basically a euphemism for the following proposition: top management knows the results it wants to see, has no idea how to achieve them, and assigns the middle manager the twofold duty of figuring out how to perform the task and then getting it done (i.e., the boss tells what he wants, not how he wants it accomplished).

Strategy considerations

There are several reasons for the foregoing results-oriented procedure. One explanation is that the middle manager is closest to the action; therefore he has most of the data, and hence is in the best position to make the decisions relevant to translating goals into action. A second explanation states that it is a superior's privilege to push decision making down and let his subordinates sweat it out. Why should he stick his neck out when he has a subordinate to do it for him?

The implications of top management's approach, however, are more important than the explanations. First of all, the middle-level general manager is provided with a much broader *de facto* responsibility than is usually codified in job descriptions or organization charts. Consequently, he must often be more of a strategist than he realizes. It is important, therefore, that he go beyond the formal definition of his job, functioning broadly enough so that he deals explicitly with the full scope of his real responsibilities. A narrow understanding of his role, by contrast, may cause him to ignore critical tasks; he cannot assume a responsibility he does not recognize.

But with responsibility goes risk, particularly where the goals are abstract and the charter is unclear. The risk is further compounded by the many constraints, external as well as organizational, within which the middle manager operates. However, along with risk goes opportunity. As Harry Truman put it, "If you can't stand the heat, get out of the kitchen." To be a strategist rather than just an order taker is exciting, even without the job's ceremonial attributes.

Formulating strategy for translating abstract goals into concrete action requires the ability to develop plans. In doing so, the middle manager must take into account external factors of an economic, political, marketing, technological, or competitive nature. Moreover, in line with his dual role, he must achieve congruence between the goals of subordinates (whose commitment is essential) and the goals imposed by superiors (whose approval he seeks).

This strategic task is both intellectual and administrative in nature, and the communication of plans is as critical as their development. Often, communication is most effectively accomplished not through proclamation but, rather, through "teaching" the general management point of view during day-to-day activities.

Summing up, to translate goals into action the middle-level general manager must:

○ Define his job realistically and broadly.

○ Assume full responsibility for translating the abstract goals into concrete action through strategic decision making and planning, taking into account both external and organizational factors.

○ Effectively communicate his decisions and plans to both his superiors and subordinates.

From action to measurement

The middle manager must be able to translate not only from abstract guidance into concrete action but also from concrete action into abstract measurement. His superior measures success in terms of results and is less interested in *how* it has been accomplished. Consequently, the middle manager's performance is most often appraised by matching the abstract results of his actions with the abstract guidance that he has been given.

This fact of organizational life sometimes leads to misunderstanding. In one company, for example, a middle manager was unable to meet his goals, and invoked his actions to show why. Top management, however, perceived the explanations as excuses. Concrete action was not part of its measurement system.

In terms of the total equation, there can be real problems when the signals from abstract measurement contradict those from abstract guidance. Where this occurs, the translation process frequently gets reversed. Instead of starting with the abstract guidance (goals) to develop specific action, the middle manager starts with the abstract measurement (required results) and translates backward to his plan of action. Here are two illustrations:

□ In one company, top management emphasized the need for its divisions to have ample productive capacity. In the measurement of performance, however, excess capacity was looked on unfavorably. As a result, division managers added capacity very cautiously, achieving high plant-utilization ratios at the expense of lost sales (which did not show up in the measurement system).

□ And in another company, top management stressed the need for new product and market development; yet the middle managers were measured on the basis of short-term profitability. With R&D and marketing expenses reducing short-term profitability, pressures to achieve the latter created an obvious reluctance to incur the former.

Translating action into measurement involves the same skills as translating goals into action. One language is operational and involves a variety of dimensions, whereas the other is abstract and is often in terms of a single dimension. The required ability is to relate these two different languages. And when measurement and goals are contradictory, the middle manager must be able to tread a thin line between the two, sometimes making trade-offs.

Furthermore, he must cope with an additional problem: the language of corporate measurement is sometimes inadequate for measuring and guiding the activities of his subordinates. While top management typically measures the middle manager on the basis of profit and loss, the middle manager has to evaluate his subordinates in terms of different quantitative measures (such as costs, production and sales volume, number of rejects, and so on) as well as qualitative judgments (such as adequacy of the plant layout, effectiveness of the R&D effort, comprehensiveness of the marketing activities). These measures not only are different in kind and more numerous, but also require greater expertise and more intimate knowledge of specifics.

Responsibility/authority

The middle manager typically assumes full responsibility for his unit and is evaluated on the results of the total operation. There is no way to shift the blame as might be done in a functionally organized setup, where marketing could claim that production did not deliver on time or production could point the finger at marketing for not bringing in enough orders.

Like the chief executive, the middle manager has to account for the performance of others. Unlike the chief executive, however, he has only limited authority in the pursuit of his goals. He often needs cooperation from equals, say, in a centralized R&D department; and he receives solicited, or unsolicited, guidance from superiors. Thus responsibility and authority do not overlap. The former exceeds the latter.

While textbooks state categorically that such an imbalance is wrong and that responsibility should be backed up with the necessary authority, the responsibility/authority discrepancy is an inevitable fact of life where divisionalization penetrates the organization. To function effectively in this imperfect world, the middle manager must meet two requirements:

1. In spite of the limited authority, he must be willing to accept full responsibility and take action accordingly. At the same time, he should recognize that he cannot do everything himself, that he must cooperate and coordinate with

others. The ability to manage multiple relationships is critical here.

2. While he always has the opportunity to "go to court," to appeal to his superiors when cooperation from equals is not forthcoming, he should rely on this route only as a last resort or when the issue is clear-cut—preventive settle-

peaceful. Career objectives and prestige, as well as positions of influence, are at stake, and the general manager in the middle is an easy and accessible target—malcontent soldiers do not pick on the general directly; they go for his officers.

The position of the middle manager is further exposed by a measurement system requiring di-

ments, even if they involve compromises, may be preferable. By going to court, he is asking somebody higher up to stick his neck out. The fact that this "somebody" has attained a higher position probably means that he is good at *not* sticking his neck out and is unlikely to be receptive unless a middle manager picks his fights wisely, carefully, and infrequently.

Inevitable politics

Discrepancies between responsibility and authority, coupled with all of the previously discussed factors—multiple relationships, the playing-coach role, translation from goals to action and back to results—necessarily result in a structure that requires managers to coexist in a political atmosphere. There are different interests and interest groups, conflicting goals and ambitions, and positions of power and weakness.

Moreover, this coexistence is not necessarily

rect and frequent responses. To meet his goals, he needs cooperation and assistance and is therefore vulnerable to sabotage. In a political sense, he is up for reelection continuously. Thus he must possess a political sensitivity as well as the constitution to stomach pressures and conflicts. He has to be aware of the configuration of the power structure and the direction of political winds. Unfortunately, in this potentially volatile atmosphere, managers often fail to ask an obvious but key question: "Who are my friends and who are my enemies?"

A major transition

The middle manager's job is usually an individual's first try at general management. Typically, he has been selected on the basis of outstanding achievement as a functional specialist; hence his previous experience is not transferable to this new terrain. His new position represents a major transition. Fred Borch, General Electric's chairman of the board and chief executive officer, considers the step from functional to general management to be the greatest challenge of a manager's entire career.

Indeed, the skills and activities which led to success in a manager's functional career—whether marketing, manufacturing, engineering, R&D, control, or finance—are usually those of specialization, of deep involvement in a narrow area. The specialist knows more and more about less and less.

In the medical and legal professions, specialization is the usual route to excellence and eminence. The manager, too, during the early phases of his career, follows this pattern; he establishes a track record by excelling in a particular specialty. But unlike the doctor and the lawyer, his career progression pattern is brutally shifted.

Having earned his spurs as a specialist, the manager is given a new and drastically different challenge, that of excelling as a generalist. Instead of knowing more and more about less and less, he now shifts to knowing less and less about more and more.

This transition, in turn, represents a major risk. Previously, each step up the functional specialization ladder led to familiar challenges which required proven skills. Now, the challenges are new and the skills unproven. Not all managers will be able to make this transition; not all will possess the required general management skills; and in spite of earlier successes, not all will successfully meet the new challenge.

Overcoming resentment

In making his major and risky transition, the middle manager, as noted earlier, does not always face a friendly working environment; rather, he may find that his promotion has caused resentment. Some may consider themselves better qualified, because of age or seniority; they may view the new middle manager's capabilities and background as insufficient for the job. Others may resent the promoted individual because he represents an "educated elite."

Yet the new middle manager needs the support of those very people who may resent his appointment. Their cooperation is essential, and he will face constant obstacles until he has it. In overcoming this possible handicap of resentment, administrative skills and experience are of utmost importance. Unfortunately, however, these skills are typically the new middle manager's short suit; he is more often long on technical abilities and experience, which are obviously less relevant to the task.

Acclimating to new terrain

Since promotions do not always occur within the same department, the middle manager often comes from another segment of the organization. As a newcomer, he will probably be unfamiliar with his unit's history, opportunities, and problems. And obtaining facts or information to accurately diagnose the situation will not be easy, for the following reasons:

◊ While superiors have assessed the unit's performance in terms of its abstract results, the middle manager has to evaluate it in terms of concrete action. The latter is much harder to determine than the former.

◊ The middle manager will have to acquaint himself not only with the "formal" organization of his unit, but with its "informal" structure as well. While the formal structure can be found in manuals and organization charts, the informal one has to be discovered through daily activities and interpersonal relationships.

◊ Politics may color the facts given. Certain information may be deliberately withheld, while other aspects may be overemphasized.

In summary, the newcomer's fact-finding mission is difficult and hazardous, and he will be required to sift through information that is often contradictory, tough to evaluate, and not always obvious.

Furthermore, he will be dealing with a new set of people, and thus will have to establish new relationships. This is a particularly difficult challenge to the manager who not only is undertaking his first general management job but also is possibly resented as a newcomer. Since relationships cannot be ordered from above, the middle manager will have to earn his own way. He will have to gain the confidence and respect of his counterparts not by virtue of the uniform he wears, but instead by the quality of his daily activities.

Managerial acrobatics: Without essential facts and established relationships, it is difficult for a middle manager to get off to a fast start. Yet he often walks into a situation that requires quick and decisive action. In this event, he will have to walk a tightrope between (a) an early commitment based on inadequate facts and non-existing relationships and (b) indecision while he establishes his facts and relationships.

The first course of action is often preferred, since it establishes a manager's authority and image. He may also be responding to pressures that are pushing him in this direction. The risks, however, are great. Before he proceeds on such a path, it is worthwhile for him to pause and consider the long-run implications of action that precedes the establishment of facts and relationships. What, for example, are the chances of making major mistakes? While it is often argued that the wrong action is preferable to no action at all, it is important for the middle manager to get off to a good start, not just a fast one. Things that start badly usually get worse.

Experimental leadership

In making his transition, a middle manager often functions as an agent of change. He may have received his assignment from top management in order to bring about changes in his new unit, or his own ambition may push him to develop new approaches. This implies experimentation and a process of learning through trial and error. Experimentation, however, means vulnerability. The middle manager's unit, for instance, may have been chosen as the experimental laboratory for the entire organization; and, since an experiment is easier to defeat than a long-established policy, the forces of resistance mentioned earlier may be encouraged to mount opposition, or even sabotage. Where the agent of change is an inexperienced newcomer, it is particularly easy to shift blame to his shoulders.

Experimental leadership rarely permits one to move ahead at great speed in a single direction. It involves slow testing and occasional backtracking that may be viewed by subordinates as indecision and defeat. Thus, they may interpret experimental leadership as lack of leadership, withholding their support and blaming their leader for inexperience or ignorance.

Under this handicap, success may be difficult to achieve. Top executives, in such circumstances, may not always come to the rescue. They may be watching rather than supporting the experiment. This is their privilege. From their vantage point, why should they stake their reputations, possibly their careers, on the uncertain outcome of an experiment?

Thus it is unrealistic to expect rescue from above. More importantly, to judge the soundness and results of an experimental change, whether initiated from above or by the middle manager himself, an objective and neutral superior is needed. He can also act as a mutually acceptable arbiter where conflicts arise, as in situations of limited authority.

The middle manager may be better served in the long run by having such a neutral arbiter above him rather than a prejudiced ally. In the former instance, cooperation and support can be obtained through candid and open negotiation; the availability of an objective judge encourages reasonable attitudes from all parties concerned. In the latter instance, resistance from others will go "underground," which obviously makes the task of obtaining cooperation and support more difficult. A case from one large company illustrates this point:

One of the divisions had to rely heavily on a centralized R&D department for its custom-made product innovations. Conflicts arose between the market-oriented division and the technology-oriented R&D department, so the division manager took his case to superiors. A new, marketing-oriented group vice president overwhelmingly ruled in favor of the division. Subsequently, the R&D department's contributions declined because of alleged "technical difficulties" and "conflicting demands from other divisions."

Challenge & opportunity

The preceding description of the characteristics of the middle-management position portrays it as a major challenge, as indeed it is. Why would anyone want to accept such an ill-defined, open-ended, risky assignment? Yet, as I pointed out earlier, with risk goes opportunity; and with open-endedness goes a job of considerably broader scope than what is stated in the formal job description.

Why is it not possible, then, to design this job by including all the positive elements and eliminating all the drawbacks? The answer is that the drawbacks are inherent in a divisional organizational structure—they can be excluded only by eliminating the structure itself.

A divisional structure, however, is essential to the conduct of large-scale operations for a diverse range of products in a variety of countries. It also permits a large number of managers to assume general management responsibilities

early in their careers, sometimes in their early or middle thirties after less than 10 years of business experience. In contrast, the functional organization usually offers an individual manager his first attempt at general management only during his middle fifties, after some 25 to 30 years of business experience.

The choice, then, is between having a broad opportunity to assume an imperfect general management job at an early age and having a very limited opportunity to hold a "perfect" general management job late in one's career. To put it in the context of Churchill's famous statement: early in a man's career, the middle-management job is the worst assignment except for all the others. Moreover, the advantages and opportunities are many, both for the company and for the aspiring executives:

□ The chance to run one's own show at a young age, rather than having to wait for a quarter of a century, should increase the probability of advancement, as well as make a business career more exciting.

□ The shift from specialist to generalist early in one's career is less perilous, and failure is less painful, than if the shift occurs later. If a manager has spent some 25 years as a specialist, he is apt to be firmly set in his ways and will find it difficult to make a major change. A younger manager, on the other hand, should still be flexible and able to adapt more easily to a different set of job requirements. Failure is also easier to take—and to overcome—early in one's career than it is later on. (Putting a 25-year track record on the line is a major risk and one that might well destroy a man's entire career.)

□ The early shift from specialist to generalist is also less risky from the company's viewpoint. When a manager who has been a specialist for a quarter of a century is selected for the president's job, the total conduct of the company is entrusted to someone with no record in general management. It is not at all certain that a successful engineering, marketing, manufacturing, or finance vice president will turn into a first-rate general manager. In the divisional organization, however, the middle manager typically manages one of several profit centers. Thus risk is greatly reduced by entrusting to an unproven general manager only a small segment of the total enterprise.

□ A large number of general management slots in an organization enables a corporation to attract and retain many capable managers and avoids an elimination contest for a company's single general management position. This large reservoir of general managers can be transferred and promoted as new opportunities arise. Since the scarcest resource of a company is usually competent management, overcoming this hurdle may eventually constitute a major competitive advantage.

□ The middle-management phenomenon is conducive to management development and training. A manager can start in a small profit center, establish a track record there, transfer to a larger unit, and so on. Thus both the breadth and the challenge of the general management job can be increased as he moves up in the ranks. His confidence and versatility will also be enhanced, fostering personal career development as well as strengthening corporate competence.

□ Middle managers are close to the action. Leadership and coordination, therefore, take place on the battlefield rather than from distant headquarters. Decisions are made more quickly by better informed people, who can more closely monitor an action's impact and ensure its proper implementation.

Conclusion

There are some important implications that can be drawn from the characteristics of the middle-level general management job; and they affect not only the man who holds it but his superiors as well.

One common pitfall is that superiors tend to judge middle managers in terms of their own jobs. They believe that middle managers have the same opportunities, prerogatives, and power that they do and therefore should shoulder similar responsibility. This same belief is frequently shared by the middle managers themselves.

As I have attempted to show, however, the middle manager's job is quite different from that of the top-level general manager. The job itself is demanding enough. It should not be made more difficult by an incorrect understanding of its scope and characteristics.

Top management often fails to recognize that imperfection is a fact of life in the middle-management job. Furthermore, formal job descriptions frequently reflect sacred dogmas like overlapping authority and responsibility. Such ostrich-like attitudes create unrealistic expectations among all parties involved. Unrealistic expectations inevitably produce disenchantments and failures. Reality, even though it may not correspond to the demands of theoretical elegance, must be faced. If reality imposes imperfection, as it does, then imperfection must be recognized and accepted, rather than swept under the rug.

Need for ratification

Given his job's characteristics, the middle manager can govern effectively only with the consent of those being governed. While he is formally promoted or demoted by his superior, the jury usually consists of his subordinates and peers. By giving or withholding their support, they greatly influence the middle manager's career.

This need for ratification is easily overlooked or underestimated by the middle manager. He may approach his job with supreme confidence in his own abilities, viewing his new appointment as evidence of his importance and talents. Where change is required, he may see himself as the new leader destined to bring order out of chaos and turn failure into success.

At the same time, he may see his subordinates as old-timers who have failed in the past to meet the challenge. Hence he may doubt their abilities and downgrade their importance. A middle manager who approaches his job by overestimating his own importance and underestimating that of his subordinates is erecting a self-imposed barrier to ratification. He is creating the conditions for a self-fulfilling prophecy—with himself as the ultimate victim.

Accommodation & compromise

Another important implication for the middle manager is the necessity of finding his way in a maze of accommodation and compromise. He cannot always make quick decisions, take a straightforward course of action, or follow completely rational and logical solutions. He must bring what he judges as necessary within the realm of what is possible.

Often it is difficult to adjust to such a complex challenge. While he may have made his mark as a technical expert whose previous successes were based on purely rational solutions to technical problems, optimization may not be the most successful approach in his new role. Rarely do perfect solutions exist for the middle manager. There are *viable* solutions, however, and they require constant accommodation and compromise.

Job strategy

Given the difficulty and challenge of general management at middle organizational levels, the job should be approached as explicitly as possible. The middle manager must attempt to define the following:

○ The scope of his multiple relationships within the organizational structure as well as the specific people to whom he must relate.

○ The "playing coach" role.

○ The "bilingual" task of translating goals to action and action to measurement.

○ The implications of having full responsibility while holding limited authority.

○ The "political" environment in which he has to survive from a position of limited power and great vulnerability.

Just as companies formulate corporate strategy by matching their resources to their environment, so can the middle manager formulate his job strategy—he can identify his total organizational environment and match this with his strengths and weaknesses as well as his personal values.

Looking at his job in strategic terms should help him face varied daily challenges, overcome frustrations, and develop a consistent pattern of behavior. Obviously, a job strategy should be not a ceremonial proclamation but, instead, a plan of action which the middle manager "carries in his back pocket" to guide him in his daily actions.

A managerial record, like a judicial one, is established through the cumulative impact of a series of decisions, many of which set precedents. If these decisions can be related not only to the specific demands of each separate issue but also to an overall philosophy and master plan, their internal consistency and cumulative impact will establish a strong and cohesive organizational fabric. This is the landmark of an effective and successful manager.

Reprint 72212

The New Managerial Work

by Rosabeth Moss Kanter

Managerial work is undergoing such enormous and rapid change that many managers are reinventing their profession as they go. With little precedent to guide them, they are watching hierarchy fade away and the clear distinctions of title, task, department, even corporation, blur. Faced with extraordinary levels of complexity and interdependency, they watch traditional sources of power erode and the old motivational tools lose their magic.

The cause is obvious. Competitive pressures are forcing corporations to adopt new flexible strategies and structures. Many of these are familiar: acquisitions and divestitures aimed at more focused combinations of business activities, reductions in management staff and levels of hierarchy, increased use of performance-based rewards. Other strategies are less common but have an even more profound effect. In a growing number of companies, for example, horizontal ties between peers are replacing vertical ties as channels of activity and communication. Companies are asking corporate staffs and functional departments to play a more strategic role with greater cross-departmental collaboration. Some orga-

Rosabeth Moss Kanter holds the Class of 1960 Chair as Professor of Business Administration at the Harvard Business School and concentrates on innovation and entrepreneurship in established companies. Her most recent book is When Giants Learn to Dance: Mastering the Challenges of Strategy, Management, and Careers in the 1990s (Simon & Schuster, 1989).

nizations are turning themselves nearly inside out —buying formerly internal services from outside suppliers, forming strategic alliances and supplier-customer partnerships that bring external relationships inside where they can influence company policy and practice. I call these emerging practices "postentrepreneurial" because they involve the application of entrepreneurial creativity and flexibility to established businesses.

Such changes come highly recommended by the experts who urge organizations to become leaner, less bureaucratic, more entrepreneurial. But so far, theorists have given scant attention to the dramatically altered realities of managerial work in these transformed corporations. We don't even have good words to describe the new relationships. "Superiors" and "subordinates" hardly seem accurate, and even "bosses" and "their people" imply more control and ownership than managers today actually possess. On top of it all, career paths are no longer straightforward and predictable but have become idiosyncratic and confusing.

Some managers experience the new managerial work as a loss of power because much of their authority used to come from hierarchical position. Now that everything seems negotiable by everyone, they are confused about how to mobilize and motivate staff. For other managers, the shift in roles and tasks offers greater personal power. The following case histories illustrate the responses of three managers in

The New Managerial Quandaries

■ At American Express, the CEO instituted a program called "One Enterprise" to encourage collaboration between different lines of business. One Enterprise has led to a range of projects where peers from different divisions work together on such synergistic ventures as cross-marketing, joint purchasing, and cooperative product and market innovation. Employees' rewards are tied to their One Enterprise efforts. Executives set goals and can earn bonuses for their contributions to results in other divisions.

☐ But how do department managers control their people when they're working on cross-departmental teams? And who determines the size of the rewards when the interests of more than one area are involved?

■ At Security Pacific National Bank, internal departments have become forces in the external marketplace. For example, the bank is involved in a joint venture with local auto dealers to sell fast financing for car purchases. And the MIS department is now a profit center selling its services inside and outside the bank.

☐ But what is the role of bank managers accountable for the success of such entrepreneurial ventures? And how do they shift their orientation from the role of boss in a chain of command to the role of customer?

■ At Digital Equipment Corporation, emphasis on supplier partnerships to improve quality and innovation has multiplied the need for cross-functional as well as cross-company collaboration. Key suppliers are included on product planning teams with engineering, manufacturing, and purchasing staff. Digital uses its human resources staff to train and do performance appraisals of its suppliers, as if they were part of the company. In cases where suppliers are also customers, purchasing and marketing departments also need to work collaboratively.

☐ But how do managers learn enough about other functions to be credible, let alone influential, members of such teams? How do they maintain adequate communication externally while staying on top of what their own departments are doing? And how do they handle the extra work of responding to projects initiated by other areas?

■ At Banc One, a growing reliance on project teams spanning more than 70 affiliated banks has led the CEO to propose eliminating officer titles because of the lack of correlation between status as measured by title and status within the collaborative team.

☐ But then what do "rank" and "hierarchy" mean anymore, especially for people whose careers consist of a sequence of projects rather than a sequence of promotions? What does "career" mean? Does it have a shape? Is there a ladder?

■ At Alcan, which is trying to find new uses and applications for its core product, aluminum, managers and professionals from line divisions form screening teams to consider and refine new-venture proposals. A venture manager, chosen from the screening team, takes charge of concepts that pass muster, drawing on Alcan's worldwide resources to build the new business. In one case of global synergy, Alcan created a new product for the Japanese market using Swedish and American technology and Canadian manufacturing capacity.

☐ But why should senior managers release staff to serve on screening and project teams for new businesses when their own businesses are making do with fewer and fewer people? How do functionally oriented managers learn enough about worldwide developments to know when they might have something of value to offer someplace else? And how do the managers of these new ventures ever go back to the conventional line organization as middle managers once their venture has been folded into an established division?

■ At IBM, an emphasis on customer partnerships to rebuild market share is leading to practices quite new to the company. In some cases, IBM has formed joint development teams with customers, where engineers from both companies share proprietary data. In others, the company has gone beyond selling equipment to actually managing a customer's management information system. Eastman Kodak has handed its U.S. data center operations to IBM to consolidate and manage, which means lower fixed costs for Kodak and a greater ability to focus on its core businesses rather than on ancillary services. Some 300 former Kodak people still fill Kodak's needs as IBM employees, while two committees of IBM and Kodak managers oversee the partnership.

☐ But who exactly do the data center people work for? Who is in charge? And how do traditional notions of managerial authority square with such a complicated set of relationships?

three different industries to the opportunities and dilemmas of structural change.

Hank is vice president and chief engineer for a leading heavy equipment manufacturer that is moving aggressively against foreign competition. One of the company's top priorities has been to increase the speed, quality, and cost-effectiveness of product development. So Hank worked with consultants to improve collaboration between manufacturing and other functions and to create closer alliances between the company and its outside suppliers. Gradually, a highly segmented operation became an integrated process involving project teams drawn from component divisions, functional departments, and external suppliers. But along the way, there were several unusual side effects. Different areas of responsibility overlapped. Some technical and manufacturing people were co-located. Liaisons from functional areas joined the larger development teams. Most unusual of all, project teams had a lot of direct contact with higher levels of the company.

Many of the managers reporting to Hank felt these changes as a loss of power. They didn't always know what their people were doing, but they still believed they ought to know. They no longer had sole input into performance appraisals; other people from other

> New strategies challenge the old power of managers and shake hierarchy to its roots.

functions had a voice as well, and some of them knew more about employees' project performance. New career paths made it less important to please direct superiors in order to move up the functional line.

Moreover, employees often bypassed Hank's managers and interacted directly with decision makers inside and outside the company. Some of these so-called subordinates had contact with division executives and senior corporate staff, and sometimes they sat in on high-level strategy meetings to which their managers were not invited.

At first Hank thought his managers' resistance to the new process was just the normal noise associated with any change. Then he began to realize that something more profound was going on. The reorganization was challenging traditional notions about the role and power of managers and shaking traditional hierarchy to its roots. And no one could see what was taking its place.

When George became head of a major corporate department in a large bank holding company, he thought he had arrived. His title and rank were unmistakable, and his department was responsible for determining product-line policy for hundreds of bank branches and the virtual clerks—in George's eyes—who managed them. George staffed his department with MBAs and promised them rapid promotion.

Then the sand seemed to shift beneath him. Losing market position for the first time in recent memory, the bank decided to emphasize direct customer service at the branches. The people George considered clerks began to depart from George's standard policies and to tailor their services to local market conditions. In many cases, they actually demanded services and responses from George's staff, and the results of their requests began to figure in performance reviews of George's department. George's people were spending more and more time in the field with branch managers, and the corporate personnel department was even trying to assign some of George's MBAs to branch and regional posts.

To complicate matters, the bank's strategy included a growing role for technology. George felt that because he had no direct control over the information systems department, he should not be held fully accountable for every facet of product design and implementation. But fully accountable he was. He had to deploy people to learn the new technology and figure out how to work with it. Furthermore, the bank was asking product departments like George's to find ways to link existing products or develop new ones that crossed traditional categories. So George's people were often away on cross-departmental teams just when he wanted them for some internal assignment.

Instead of presiding over a tidy empire the way his predecessor had, George presided over what looked to him like chaos. The bank said senior executives should be "leaders, not managers," but George didn't know what that meant, especially since he seemed to have lost control over his subordinates' assignments, activities, rewards, and careers. He resented his perceived loss of status.

The CEO tried to show him that good results achieved the new way would bring great monetary rewards, thanks to a performance-based bonus program that was gradually replacing more modest yearly raises. But the pressures on George were also greater, unlike anything he'd ever experienced.

For Sally, purchasing manager at an innovative computer company, a new organizational strategy was a gain rather than a loss, although it changed her relationship with the people reporting to her. Less than ten years out of college, she was hired as an analyst—a semiprofessional, semiclerical job—then promoted to a purchasing manager's job in a sleepy staff department. She didn't expect to go much further in what was then a well-established hierarchy. But after a shocking downturn, top management encouraged employees to rethink traditional ways of doing things. Sally's boss, the head of purchasing, suggested that "partnerships" with key suppliers might improve quality, speed innovation, and reduce costs.

Soon Sally's backwater was at the center of policymaking, and Sally began to help shape strategy. She organized meetings between her company's senior executives and supplier CEOs. She sent her staff to contribute supplier intelligence at company semi-

> ## In the new organization, it's hard to tell the managers from the nonmanagers.

nars on technical innovation, and she spent more of her own time with product designers and manufacturing planners. She led senior executives on a tour of supplier facilities, traveling with them in the corporate jet.

Because some suppliers were also important customers, Sally's staff began meeting frequently with marketing managers to share information and address joint problems. Sally and her group were now also acting as internal advocates for major suppliers. Furthermore, many of these external companies now contributed performance appraisals of Sally and her team, and their opinions weighed almost as heavily as those of her superiors.

As a result of the company's new direction, Sally felt more personal power and influence, and her ties to peers in other areas and to top management were stronger. But she no longer felt like a manager directing subordinates. Her staff had become a pool of resources deployed by many others besides Sally. She was exhilarated by her personal opportunities but not quite sure the people she managed should have the same freedom to choose their own assignments. After all, wasn't that a manager's prerogative?

Hank's, George's, and Sally's very different stories say much about the changing nature of managerial work. However hard it is for managers at the very top to remake strategy and structure, they themselves will probably retain their identity, status, and control. For the managers below them, structural change is often much harder. As work units become more participative and team oriented, and as professionals and knowledge workers become more prominent, the distinction between manager and nonmanager begins to erode.

To understand what managers must do to achieve results in the postentrepreneurial corporation, we need to look at the changing picture of how such companies operate. The picture has five elements:

1. There are a greater number and variety of channels for taking action and exerting influence.

2. Relationships of influence are shifting from the vertical to the horizontal, from chain of command to peer networks.

3. The distinction between managers and those managed is diminishing, especially in terms of information, control over assignments, and access to external relationships.

4. External relationships are increasingly important as sources of internal power and influence, even of career development.

5. As a result of the first four changes, career development has become less intelligible but also less circumscribed. There are fewer assured routes to success, which produces anxiety. At the same time, career paths are more open to innovation, which produces opportunity.

To help companies implement their competitive organizational strategies, managers must learn new ways to manage, confronting changes in their own bases of power and recognizing the need for new ways to motivate people.

The Bases of Power

The changes I've talked about can be scary for people like George and the managers reporting to Hank, who were trained to know their place, to follow orders, to let the company take care of their careers, to do things by the book. The book is gone. In the new corporation, managers have only themselves to count on for success. They must learn to operate without the crutch of hierarchy. Position, title, and authority are no longer adequate tools, not in a world where subordinates are encouraged to think for themselves and where managers have to work synergistically with other departments and even other companies. Success depends increasingly on tapping into sources of good ideas, on figuring out whose collaboration is needed to act on those ideas, on working with both to produce results. In short, the new managerial work implies very different ways of obtaining and using power.

The postentrepreneurial corporation is not only leaner and flatter, it also has many more channels for action. Cross-functional projects, business-unit joint ventures, labor-management forums, innovation funds that spawn activities outside mainstream budgets and reporting lines, strategic partnerships with suppliers or customers – these are all overlays on the traditional organization chart, strategic pathways that ignore the chain of command.

Their existence has several important implications. For one thing, they create more potential centers of power. As the ways to combine resources increase, the ability to command diminishes. Alternative paths of communication, resource access, and execution erode the authority of those in the nominal chain of command. In other words, the opportunity for greater speed and flexibility undermines hierarchy. As more and more strategic action takes place in these channels, the jobs that focus inward on particular departments decline in power.

As a result, the ability of managers to get things done depends more on the number of networks in which they're centrally involved than on their height in a hierarchy. Of course, power in any organization always has a network component, but rank and formal structure used to be more limiting. For example, access to information and the ability to get informal backing were often confined to the few officially sanctioned contact points between departments or between the company and its vendors or customers. Today these official barriers are disappearing, while so-called informal networks grow in importance.

In the emerging organization, managers add value by deal making, by brokering at interfaces, rather than by presiding over their individual empires. It was traditionally the job of top executives or specialists to scan the business environment for new ideas, opportunities, and resources. This kind of environmental scanning is now an important part of a manager's job at every level and in every function. And the environment to be scanned includes various company divisions, many potential outside partners, and large parts of the world. At the same time, people are encouraged to think about what they know that might have value elsewhere. An engineer designing windshield wipers, for example, might discover properties of rubber adhesion to glass that could be useful in other manufacturing areas.

Every manager must think cross-functionally because every department has to play a strategic role, understanding and contributing to other facets of the business. In Hank's company, the technical managers and staff working on design engineering used to concentrate only on their own areas of expertise. Under the new system, they have to keep in mind what manufacturing does and how it does it. They need to visit plants and build relationships so they can ask informed questions.

One multinational corporation, eager to extend the uses of its core product, put its R&D staff and lab-oratory personnel in direct contact with marketing experts to discuss lines of research. Similarly, the superior economic track record of Raytheon's New Products Center – dozens of new products and patents yielding profits many times their development costs – derives from the connections it builds between its inventors and the engineering and marketing staffs of the business units it serves.

This strategic and collaborative role is particularly important for the managers and professionals on corporate staffs. They need to serve as integrators and facilitators, not as watchdogs and interventionists. They need to sell their services, justify themselves to the business units they serve, literally compete with outside suppliers. General Foods recently put overhead charges for corporate staff services on a pay-as-you-use basis. Formerly, these charges were either assigned uniformly to users and nonusers alike, or the services were mandatory. Product managers sometimes had to work through as many as eight layers of management and corporate staff to get business

To add value, managers think and work across boundaries.

plans approved. Now these staffs must prove to the satisfaction of their internal customers that their services add value.

By contrast, some banks still have corporate training departments that do very little except get in the way. They do no actual training, for example, yet they still exercise veto power over urgent divisional training decisions and consultant contracts.

As managers and professionals spend more time working across boundaries with peers and partners over whom they have no direct control, their negotiating skills become essential assets. Alliances and partnerships transform impersonal, arm's-length contracts into relationships involving joint planning and joint decision making. Internal competitors and adversaries become allies on whom managers depend for their own success. At the same time, more managers at more levels are active in the kind of external diplomacy that only the CEO or selected staffs used to conduct.

In the collaborative forums that result, managers are more personally exposed. It is trust that makes partnerships work. Since collaborative ventures often bring together groups with different methods, cultures, symbols, even languages, good deal making depends on empathy – the ability to step into other people's shoes and appreciate their goals. This applies not only to intricate global joint ventures but also to the efforts of engineering and manufacturing to work together more effectively. Effective communication in a cooperative effort rests on more than a simple exchange of information; people must be adept at anticipating the responses of other groups. "Before I get too excited about our department's design ideas," an engineering manager told me, "I'm learning to ask myself, 'What's the marketing position on this? What

> ## Today's executive must bargain, negotiate, and sell ideas like any other politician.

will manufacturing say?' That sometimes forces me to make changes before I even talk to them."

An increase in the number of channels for strategic contact within the postentrepreneurial organization means more opportunities for people with ideas or information to trigger action: salespeople encouraging account managers to build strategic partnerships with customers, for example, or technicians searching for ways to tap new-venture funds to develop software. Moreover, top executives who have to spend more time on cross-boundary relationships are forced to delegate more responsibility to lower level managers. Delegation is one more blow to hierarchy, of course, since subordinates with greater responsibility are bolder about speaking up, challenging authority, and charting their own course.

For example, it is common for new-venture teams to complain publicly about corporate support departments and to reject their use in favor of external service providers, often to the consternation of more orthodox superiors. A more startling example occured in a health care company where members of a task force charged with finding synergies among three lines of business shocked corporate executives by criticizing upper management behavior in their report. Service on the task force had created collective awareness of a shared problem and had given people the courage to confront it.

The search for internal synergies, the development of strategic alliances, and the push for new ventures all emphasize the political side of a leader's work. Executives must be able to juggle a set of constituencies rather than control a set of subordinates. They have to bargain, negotiate, and sell instead of making unilateral decisions and issuing commands. The leader's task, as Chester Barnard recognized long ago, is to develop a network of cooperative relationships among all the people, groups, and organizations that have

something to contribute to an economic enterprise. Postentrepreneurial strategies magnify the complexity of this task. After leading Teknowledge, a producer of expert systems software, through development alliances with six corporations including General Motors and Procter & Gamble, company chairman Lee Hecht said he felt like the mayor of a small city. "I have a constituency that won't quit. It takes a hell of a lot of balancing." The kind of power achieved through a network of stakeholders is very different from the kind of power managers wield in a traditional bureaucracy. The new way gets more done, but it also takes more time. And it creates an illusion about freedom and security.

The absence of day-to-day constraints, the admonition to assume responsibility, the pretense of equality, the elimination of visible status markers, the prevalence of candid dialogues across hierarchical levels—these can give employees a false sense that all hierarchy is a thing of the past. Yet at the same time, employees still count on hierarchy to shield them when things go wrong. This combination would create the perfect marriage of freedom and support—freedom when people want to take risks, support when the risks don't work out.

In reality, less benevolent combinations are also possible, combinations not of freedom and support but of insecurity and loss of control. There is often a pretense in postentrepreneurial companies that sta-

> ## The promise of freedom has a dark side: insecurity and loss of control.

tus differences have nothing to do with power, that the deference paid to top executives derives from their superior qualifications rather than from the power they have over the fates of others. But the people at the top of the organization chart still wield power—and sometimes in ways that managers below them experience as arbitrary. Unprecedented individual freedom also applies to top managers, who are now free to make previously unimaginable deals, order unimaginable cuts, or launch unimaginable takeovers. The reorganizations that companies undertake in their search for new synergies can uncover the potential unpredictability and capriciousness of corporate careers. A man whose company was undergoing drastic restructuring told me, "For all of my ownership share and strategic centrality and voice in decisions, I can still be faced with a shift in direction not of my own making. I can still be reorganized into a corner. I can still be relocated into oblivion. I can still be reviewed out of my special project budget."

These realities of power, change, and job security are important because they affect the way people view their leaders. When the illusion of simultaneous freedom and protection fades, the result can be a loss of motivation.

Sources of Motivation

One of the essential, unchanging tasks of leaders is to motivate and guide performance. But motivational tools are changing fast. More and more businesses are doing away with the old bureaucratic incentives and using entrepreneurial opportunity to attract the best talent. Managers must exercise more leadership even as they watch their bureaucratic power slip away. Leadership, in short, is more difficult yet more critical than ever.

Because of the unpredictability of even the most benign restructuring, managers are less able to guarantee a particular job—or any job at all—no matter what a subordinate's performance level. The reduction in hierarchical levels curtails a manager's ability to promise promotion. New compensation systems that make bonuses and raises dependent on objective performance measures and on team appraisals deprive managers of their role as the sole arbiter of higher pay. Cross-functional and cross-company teams can rob managers of their right to direct or even understand the work their so-called subordinates do. In any case, the shift from routine work, which was amenable to oversight, to "knowledge" work, which often is not, erodes a manager's claim to superior expertise. And partnerships and ventures that put lower level people in direct contact with each other across departmental and company boundaries cut heavily into the managerial monopoly on information. At a consumer packaged-goods manufacturer that replaced several levels of hierarchy with teams, plant team members in direct contact with the sales force often had data on product ordering trends before the higher level brand managers who set product policy.

As if the loss of carrots and sticks was not enough, many managers can no longer even give their people clear job standards and easily mastered procedural rules. Postentrepreneurial corporations seek problem-solving, initiative-taking employees who will go the unexpected extra mile for the customer. To complicate the situation further still, the complexities of work in the new organization—projects and relationships clamoring for attention in every direction—exacerbate the feeling of overload.

With the old motivational tool kit depleted, leaders need new and more effective incentives to encourage high performance and build commitment. There are five new tools:

Mission. Helping people believe in the importance of their work is essential, especially when other forms of certainty and security have disappeared. Good leaders can inspire others with the power and excitement of their vision and give people a sense of purpose and pride in their work. Pride is often a better source of motivation than the traditional corporate career ladder and the promotion-based reward system. Technical professionals, for example, are often motivated most effectively by the desire to see their work contribute to an excellent final product.

Agenda Control. As career paths lose their certainty and companies' futures grow less predictable, people can at least be in charge of their own professional lives. More and more professionals are passing up jobs with glamour and prestige in favor of jobs that give them greater control over their own activities and direction. Leaders give their subordinates this opportunity when they give them release time to work on pet projects, when they emphasize results instead of procedures, and when they delegate work and the decisions about how to do it. Choice of their next project is a potent reward for people who perform well.

Share of Value Creation. Entrepreneurial incentives that give teams a piece of the action are highly appropriate in collaborative companies. Because extra rewards are based only on measurable results, this approach also conserves resources. Innovative companies are experimenting with incentives like phantom stock for development of new ventures and other strategic achievements, equity participation in project returns, and bonuses pegged to key performance targets. Given the cross-functional nature of many projects today, rewards of this kind must sometimes be systemwide, but individual managers can also ask for a bonus pool for their own areas, contingent, of course, on meeting performance goals. And everyone can share the kinds of rewards that are abundant and free—awards and recognition.

Learning. The chance to learn new skills or apply them in new arenas is an important motivator in a turbulent environment because it's oriented toward securing the future. "The learning organization" promises to become a 1990s business buzzword as companies seek to learn more systematically from their experience and to encourage continuous learning for their people. In the world of high technology, where people understand uncertainty, the attractiveness of any company often lies in its capacity to provide learning and experience. By this calculus, access to training, mentors, and challenging projects is more important than pay or benefits. Some prominent companies – General Electric, for example – have always been able to attract top talent, even when they could not promise upward mobility, because people see them as a training ground, a good place to learn, and a valuable addition to a résumé.

Reputation. Reputation is a key resource in professional careers, and the chance to enhance it can be an outstanding motivator. The professional's reliance on reputation stands in marked contrast to the bureaucrat's anonymity. Professionals have to make a name for themselves, while traditional corporate managers and employees stayed behind the scenes. Indeed, the accumulation of reputational "capital" provides not only an immediate ego boost but also the kind of publicity that can bring other rewards, even other job offers. Managers can enhance reputation – and improve motivation – by creating stars, by providing abundant public recognition and visible awards, by crediting the authors of innovation, by publicizing people outside their own departments, and by plugging people into organizational and professional networks.

The new, collaborative organization is predicated on a logic of flexible work assignments, not of fixed job responsibilities. To promote innovation and responsiveness, two of today's competitive imperatives, managers need to see this new organization as a

> When an engineer saw a TV ad for his design, he shouted to his family, "Hey! That's mine!" *That's* compensation.

cluster of activity sets, not as a rigid structure. The work of leadership in this new corporation will be to organize both sequential and synchronous projects of varying length and breadth, through which varying combinations of people will move, depending on the tasks, challenges, and opportunities facing the area and its partners at any given moment.

Leaders need to carve out projects with tangible accomplishments, milestones, and completion dates and then delegate responsibility for these projects to the people who flesh them out. Clearly delimited projects can counter overload by focusing effort and can provide short-term motivation when the fate of

the long-term mission is uncertain. Project responsibility leads to ownership of the results and sometimes substitutes for other forms of reward. In companies where product development teams define and run their own projects, members commonly say that the greatest compensation they get is seeing the advertisements for their products. "Hey, that's mine! I did that!" one engineer told me he trumpeted to his family the first time he saw a commercial for his group's innovation.

This sense of ownership, along with a definite time frame, can spur higher levels of effort. Whenever people are engaged in creative or problem-solving projects that will have tangible results by deadline dates, they tend to come in at all hours, to think about the project in their spare time, to invest in it vast sums of physical and emotional energy. Knowing that the project will end and that completion will be an occasion for reward and recognition makes it possible to work much harder.

Leaders in the new organization do not lack motivational tools, but the tools are different from those of traditional corporate bureaucrats. The new rewards are based not on status but on contribution, and they consist not of regular promotion and automatic pay raises but of excitement about mission and a share of the glory and the gains of success. The new security is not employment security (a guaranteed job no matter what) but *employability* security – increased value in the internal and external labor markets. Commitment to the organization still matters, but today managers build commitment by offering project opportunities. The new loyalty is not to the boss or to the company but to projects that actualize a mission and offer challenge, growth, and credit for results.

The old bases of managerial authority are eroding, and new tools of leadership are taking their place. Managers whose power derived from hierarchy and who were accustomed to a limited area of personal control are learning to shift their perspectives and widen their horizons. The new managerial work consists of looking outside a defined area of responsibility to sense opportunities and of forming project teams drawn from any relevant sphere to address them. It involves communication and collaboration across functions, across divisions, and across companies whose activities and resources overlap. Thus rank, title, or official charter will be less important factors in success at the new managerial work than having the knowledge, skills, and sensitivity to mobilize people and motivate them to do their best. ▽

Reprint 89606

The wagon trains demanded leadership. Ward Bond was a great manager.

Wagon Masters and Lesser Managers
by J.S. NINOMIYA

Over the past several years, I've seen more and more books and articles about managerial effectiveness and how it can increase productivity. I've also seen more and more companies try to improve executive skills through education programs, sensitivity training, and participatory management. Yet at the same time I see businesses continuing to promote people into administrative ranks with apparently little consideration for their ability to manage others, their willingness to include subordinates in decision making, or their suitability as teachers and role models for a coming generation of supervisors. Many of these newly promoted managers perform in the managerial styles of a past era, characterized by self-serving attitudes, empire building, and autocratic methods. Eventually they too need sensitivity training and remedial seminars to try to correct their ineffective behavior.

In short, too many companies are making the same mistake with managers that the auto industry used to make with quality: build it now, fix it later. We've finally started building automobiles right in the first place. Now we need to do the same with managers: hire and promote the right men and women to begin with instead of trying to "fix" them years later after they've done their damage.

I am neither a social scientist nor a management consultant. For the last 20 years, I've worked at middle management jobs in the auto industry, where I have supervised many people and worked for many supervisors. In addition, I worked on a research team in the 1970s that took me into the offices of colleagues in the oil and auto industries, and there, for weeks at a time, I was able to watch managerial behavior in other companies from a fly-on-the-wall perspective. In my experience, it is rare that managers are selected for their supervisory ability. Indeed, most of those I've known lacked what I consider the most basic requirements for effective management – an understanding of the human condition and an appreciation of people. Most managers today are still selected solely on the basis of business expertise or success in nonsupervisory positions, and the styles they develop are inadequate, to say the least.

It may help to describe some of these styles. Here are seven I meet regularly:

The Godfather. Despite the current emphasis on teamwork and participatory management, the Godfather style still prevails. Godfathers typically demand complete control of their organizations and total loyalty from their employees. Subordinates are given freedom in their routine duties, but their goals are dictated from above. A Godfather's image and ego require frequent nurturing, usually in the form of successful confrontations with outsiders. To be recognized as good employees, subordinates need only stand at ringside and root for the boss.

People who have been subjected to this style for many years rarely become good managers themselves. Most often they become new Godfathers. At the opposite extreme, they become submissive and ineffectual.

Groups led by Godfathers are normally goal oriented and known for getting things done. Outsiders see them as well-oiled machines. Superiors depend on them. Because they rely on one person for nearly all decisions, however, the goals of Godfather groups are often self-serving and not always in the best interests of the organization as a whole.

The Ostrich. Ostriches love the status quo and fear discord. They always hope problems will simply go away and would rather stick their heads in the sand than face unpleasantness of any kind.

Ostriches believe firmly in nonconfrontational approaches to problem solving, and they avoid issues and debate. They are often capable and knowledgeable in their own areas of expertise, but they are usually better suited to serve as assistants than as managers. The fact is, progress cannot be achieved without conflict, and a preference for the status quo stifles growth and can weaken morale. Ostriches are more concerned with a superior's opinion of their job performance than with the morale of their subordinates, who often lack initiative, imagination, and productivity, especially if they've had their Ostrich managers for a long time.

The Do-It-Yourselfer. Do-It-Yourselfers want to handle everything themselves, especially the more challenging assignments. The only tasks they ordinarily delegate are the ones that they find trivial or that require special skills. They are often capable

In his 27 years at Ford, J.S. Ninomiya has held a variety of line, research, and management positions. He is currently safety planning manager for the company's environmental and safety engineering staff.

individuals; many are workaholics. All live by the motto: "If you want a job done well, do it yourself!" They spend long hours at their jobs and are seen by upper management as candidates for promotion.

Unfortunately, they often make themselves indispensable. In several cases I know, a Do-It-Yourselfer's sudden illness has brought an entire department to a standstill. In addition, people who work for them often react like the people who work for Ostriches. Unable to get recognition and challenging assignments, they turn into mere hired hands. If the goals of an organization include productivity improvement and personnel development, then Godfathers, Ostriches, and Do-It-Yourselfers make poor managers.

The Detailer. Detailers want to know everything their subordinates do "in detail." In larger organizations, Detailers are so busy trying to keep up with their employees that they are virtually incapable of managing groups of any size. As they see it, their task is to be wiser and know more than their subordinates, so that they can make correct decisions by themselves. Detailers don't like group decisions and find delegating difficult. When they do delegate, they stay constantly in touch to make sure that subordinates do not arrive at independent decisions. Detailers generally lack confidence in others and make subordinates redo assignments again and again.

The decisions made by Detailers are often good ones, but they are rarely prompt. Since the usefulness of a decision is seldom a function of the time it takes to make it, a good but leisurely decision is often too late to be useful. Detailers are best suited for supervising small groups that can afford to work slowly.

The Politician. Many of us like to work for Politicians because they tell us what we want to hear. Their superiors like having them around for the same reason. One of the drawbacks to this style is that Politicians tend to overdo it. A colleague of mine received 37 notes of commendation in one year, though the boss who sent them rated his overall performance average. Praise of this kind produces nothing but frustration and resentment. No one looks forward to the 38th insincere note from the boss.

Another drawback is that Politicians tend to stratify employees and management. On hearing objections from his or her own boss, for example, the Politician may abruptly overturn a decision previously approved by subordinates. What passes for managerial skill is nothing more than a talent for dodging bullets. Politicians with fast reflexes may succeed for a while, but few manage to dodge forever.

The Arbitrator. Arbitrators are often very successful at dealing with large groups because they possess a deep understanding of people and human conflict. They believe in teamwork and team decisions. If an organization's goal is to promote harmony and increase productivity, then this style is effective, especially in mid-management ranks. On the other hand, if what the organization needs is a vocal spokesperson and a competitive leader, then the Arbitrator may not meet the need. Arbitrators are usually personable and well liked, but they do have a weakness for compromise at the wrong moment, and they tend to be so friendly with subordinates that they find it hard to crack down when the going gets tough.

The Eager Beaver. In the same way that beavers build ever larger dams to interrupt the flow of water, so Eager Beavers create ever greater workloads and eventually interrupt the smooth functioning of their organizations. These managers measure their worth by the number of letters and reports they generate and by how hard their subordinates work. They are seldom content unless their subordinates put in overtime and work weekends at least occasionally. In many cases, even those who don't need to put in overtime are pressured into it. In my experience, unnecessary work

The Godfather's heavyweight ego puts him in the center of the ring.

The Ostrich's fear of discord leaves conflict unresolved.

demoralizes employees, and constant work pressure wears them down.

Many managers of the past were Eager Beavers and Godfathers who rationalized hiring more and more employees on the grounds of minimizing overtime expenditures. But the fact is, these empire builders don't change their habits even when their departments double in size. Eager Beavers and Godfathers did so much empire building at Ford between 1979 and 1982 that new management was able to cut back the number of employees by more than one-third without affecting productivity.

On the positive side, Eager Beavers are thorough. On the negative side, they produce a mass of useless information that often gets filed in wastebaskets.

A catalog of management styles could go on and on, but these seven styles, singly or in combination, describe more than three-quarters of all the managers I've known and many I have worked for. Every one of them meets some of the needs of an organization some of the time, but not one of them is what I would call an effective manager. Six of the seven types have more weaknesses than strengths, and they all train subordinates in their own inadequate image.

The effective manager is more difficult to describe, for the very reason that he or she refuses to be typecast. The trouble with most of us is not that we sometimes act like, say, Godfathers, but that we act like Godfathers all the time. An effective manager is sometimes a Godfather and sometimes a Do-It-Yourselfer, often an Arbitrator and occasionally even an Ostrich. After 27 years, I think I know good managers when I see them, and I think I know what it is they do. I even think I know how to find them. Let me illustrate with one of my favorite examples.

Some of the most effective managers this country has ever seen were the wagon masters of the west-ward movement in the last century. A wagon master had two jobs. He had to keep the wagons moving toward their destination day after day despite all obstacles. He also had to maintain harmony and a spirit of teamwork among the members of his party and to resolve daily problems before they became divisive. A wagon master's worth was measured by his ability to reach the destination safely and to keep spirits high along the way. He had to do both in order to do either. I see the skills of effective managers as essentially the same, and I can sum them up in the roles they play:

Decision Maker. To begin with, effective managers are decisive. Despite all our newfound emphasis on teamwork and consensus, decision-making ability is by far the most important tool a manager needs on a daily basis. Teamwork is right for many decisions. Managers alone must make many others, including most of those involving job assignments, people, and interorganizational disputes. But here as elsewhere, an executive's responsibility is twofold—to make the right decision but also to encourage subordinate participation. In my experience the best policy is to involve as many employees as practical, to present them with the whole issue to be resolved (not just pieces of it), to sincerely seek and appreciate their suggestions, and throughout the process, to display the kind of decisiveness it would take to act alone.

Listener and Communicator. Many managers hear their subordinates but do not "listen." It takes enormous effort to get to know employees individually and to learn how to sense the group dynamics in an organization. A supervisor, like the leader of a wagon train, must be sensitive to moods and attitudes. By listening and communicating well, managers can fulfill the basic human need employees have to be recognized and appreciated. Good listening is also part of an effective style in meetings. The successful managers I've known never dominate the table but let everyone express his or her views.

Teacher. One of the responsibilities of a good manager is to train subordinates to become managers. This does not mean having one or two favorites who are seen as anointed successors. It means training everyone who has potential. There are many ways to help people learn to make decisions: delegate responsibility, even to the lowest ranks; include subordinates where feasible in every project; hold regular discussion sessions; let employees represent the company with outside contacts. The effective managers I've known use all these ways of building positive self-images in their employees.

Indeed, good managers all seem to have one thing in common: they delegate well, and trusting people to do the right thing, give minimal direction. They don't reprimand subordinates who fail but encourage them to try again and to seek the help of coworkers and their own subordinates whenever possible. Good supervisors rarely find themselves burdened with unimaginative staff work because they constantly challenge the limits of their subordinates' creativity.

Peacemaker. Effective managers know how to minimize conflict. Some supervisors simply ignore its existence or become abusive and threaten to dismiss everyone involved. But managers who want their organizations to function productively face day-to-day problems directly. One way is to confront employees in order to determine the causes of conflict. Another is to encourage work groups like quality circles; a third is to rotate jobs and reassign people. Every workplace has conflicts. Effective managers sense them early and deal with them head-on.

Visionary. Wagon masters pushed their wagons toward specific destinations—Oregon, the California gold fields. Effective managers set goals that are just as firm and meaningful. Identifying goals is no less important than creating the means to achieve them. We have all looked for a car in a crowded parking lot. We trudge up one aisle and down the next, growing increasingly frustrated and embarrassed. Any clear sense of where we had left the car would have saved us enormous time and energy. In an effective organization, collective as well as individual goals are well defined and understood. Good managers never let themselves or their subordinates lose sight of them.

Self-Critic. How many times have you heard the expression "The boss is always right" or "The boss is the boss"? Not many managers are self-confident enough to admit their mistakes. Most believe that making mistakes is the worst corporate offense, and they don't allow the notion of human error to enter their philosophies. In fact, some insist on having their way even when they know they're wrong. Worse yet, subordinates who recognize the boss's mistakes can't correct them for fear of reprisal. Employees lose respect for their supervisors, and blunders achieve the status of doctrine. Effective manag-

The Politician's relentless insincerity wears subordinates down.

ers are quick to admit their own mistakes and don't dwell on the mistakes of others. They want to learn from mistakes so as not to repeat them. They know that while assessing damage and causes is often important, assigning blame is not.

Team Captain. Consensus decision making is one of the most powerful tools at a manager's disposal. Working alone, executives may find it difficult to make decisions affecting the whole organization — retooling a plant, reorganizing departments, even remodeling office space — because they are so often limited by the self-serving and conflicting information arriving from different departments. Teamwork decisions can minimize mistakes in such situations and ward off much dissatisfaction among employees whose voices would not otherwise be heard.

Leader. An executive's attitude toward subordinates is perhaps the most important trait of all. Effective managers have drive and determination, but they also have qualities like trust, modesty, politeness, patience, and sensitivity. Good managers genuinely like and appreciate people. They don't just manipulate or command; they lead. And they understand their dual function. Getting the wagons to Oregon without the passengers is no achievement. Keeping everyone in high spirits right up to the moment they perish in the desert is not success.

The need for good managers is growing. Many companies are downsizing in an effort to operate more efficiently. They are combining departments and cutting the work force but creating larger groups to be supervised. If we have fewer managers, we need them to be even more effective, which means that the ability to manage people is becoming more and more important. Yet the way we select managers hasn't changed much, and the managers we find are not much better than they ever were.

One short-term approach to the problem is to retrain today's executives. I've seen numerous efforts to introduce participatory management, promote teamwork, alter managerial attitudes, even change the so-called corporate culture. These are all moves in the right direction, but the results are often disappointing. Many people simply cannot see their own shortcomings. Others pay only lip service to such programs. Most disappointing of all, many seem to overestimate how much they've learned and changed in the course of retraining. After some recent participatory management workshops at Ford, for example, managers and their employees were asked to rate the benefits: nearly two-thirds of the executives felt they had become better supervisors, but

only a quarter of the subordinates shared that view. We must be careful not to fool ourselves with rosy self-assessments, or to believe we have solved a problem when we have really only talked about it.

For the long term, we need to make changes in the way we hire, reward, and evaluate managers. We need to improve the methods we already use — better personality profiles, better interviewing techniques, a better environment for people to work in once they've been hired. In addition, I have three unconventional suggestions:

First, abandon excessive perks. I believe effective managers always treat subordinates as people first and employees second. I know one such manager who left thank-you notes on his desk for the evening cleaning crew (who, as you might guess, kept his office immaculate). I know executives who take turns with their subordinates cleaning the office coffee maker and others who automatically pick up trash on their plants' floors instead of stepping over it. The people who work for such managers can be vehement in their unwillingness to work for anyone else.

On the other hand, I've met managers who think they are cast in a different mold from their employees — even when they all come from similar backgrounds. These executives consider themselves members of an elite and take pride in the symbols of their status, which they believe will increase their authority and make them more effective.

In fact, perks and status symbols often act as obstacles to good management. After many years of enjoying these rewards, some managers develop such a sense of privilege that they begin to look on employee concerns and complaints as encroachments on their prerogatives.

Demonstrations of rank have nothing to do with good management; yet in the United States the practice of granting special privileges is almost universal.

I recently discussed this subject with a vice president of one of the country's largest companies. He maintained that management perks were needed to inspire people to achieve corporate goals. Without them, he felt, people would have no incentive to work harder. I agreed that perks can be useful in some cases to reward achievements. But what about the rewards of approval and self-satisfaction? He was puzzled. Who would work harder for nothing but self-satisfaction? I asked then how he justified rewarding his executives but not his workers since, in his own view, people will not perform without the prospect of rewards. He said he could not reward everyone or his company would face bankruptcy.

I suspect that this man's view — the carrot for executives, the stick, presumably, for others — is shared by many in top management. There are other industrial countries, however, where such privilege is rare, yet productivity remains high.

Several years ago, a friend of mine—an American executive at a large U.S. corporation—went to work for a Japanese company in the United States. Previously, he had been a profit-oriented manager with short-term goals and had enjoyed a wide range of perks and privileges. The last time I saw him I was astonished at the change in his outlook. He had become a respected manager of people, with long-term goals and a vision for his company's future. He no longer had all the accustomed perks. He was no longer isolated in his executive suite but spent much of his time on the factory floor.

I am not suggesting that all managers adopt the Japanese style and abandon traditional American values. I cannot say that all perks are bad business practice. Many successful companies use them, some as a means of projecting company images to outsiders.

The Eager Beaver's gnawing ambition dams up the company works.

Still, the thought of doing without them is attractive. Managers need to mix with subordinates to promote a spirit of teamwork, to nurture commitment to the job, to monitor the heartbeat of the company, and to remind themselves how well and how quickly many of their subordinates could fill their shoes.

Second, ignore narrow expertise. Common sense tells us to hire supervisors with expertise in the field they're expected to manage, but there are several drawbacks to this practice. To begin with, one of the most frequent complaints of managers themselves is that they become typecast in their particular expertise and have little opportunity to grow into other areas of business. Their promotional paths are similarly limited. But the man or woman who feels stifled by typecasting is not likely to be a truly effective manager, stimulated by new challenges, open to new ideas, creative, enthusiastic, optimistic. Moreover, expertise tends to become outdated, and in my experience this phenomenon presents two very real dangers. One is that entrenched managers will suppress innovation. Another, more dangerous possibility is that a manager with fossilized expertise may give subordinates too little room to grow.

Managers whose technical expertise is in another area will take a broader view of organizational goals, will depend more on subordinates, and will insist on teamwork, thus freeing themselves to manage people—the task for which they were hired.

In my view, the same considerations ought to apply to the old question of whether to promote from within or hire from without. Most people dislike the idea of bringing in outsiders from other companies or even transferring them from other departments. This is probably because most people fear for their own chances of promotion. But what matters is to broaden the perspectives of the organization and to find executives who can manage people. Inside or outside is irrelevant.

Third, get references from a candidate's old subordinates. This may sound radical. It is certainly unorthodox. I know of only one organization that contacted the candidate's former subordinates. Why should the references of past subordinates be less important than the references of past employers? When we hire someone to manage people, we need to know what previous employees thought. Unlike old bosses, who often write complimentary letters in behalf of people they were happy to see go, old subordinates are likely to say what they mean. There is no better judge of a supervisor's character than the people who depend on him or her to hear their complaints, arbitrate their differences, sharpen their skills, and lead them to the fulfillment of their goals.

I am convinced that the key to all our business goals—better quality, bigger sales, increased profits—is this emphasis on people. Like wagon masters, effective managers understand that their own success is inseparable from the success of their fellow travelers. Good managers get things done by caring about the people who do them.

Reprint 88209

The middle manager as innovator

If a company culture fosters collaboration and its structure encourages managers to 'do what needs to be done,' more of them are likely to be entrepreneurial

Rosabeth Moss Kanter

If there's one thing that most U.S. executives agree on, it's the need for higher productivity in American workplaces. So far most efforts at raising performance have concentrated on factory and office employees – partly, one assumes, because their output is easily measured. However, the increases in productivity at the shop or office level will mean nothing in the long run, if, for instance, new products aren't designed, new structures aren't put in place to accommodate change, or new equipment isn't conceived to improve product quality. In other words, a company's productivity depends to a great degree on how innovative its middle managers are.

In this article, the author describes a study she conducted of 165 middle managers in five companies to determine what managers contribute to innovation and what factors the most innovative companies have in common. She found that, among other things, innovative managers tend to be visionary, comfortable with change, and persistent. Innovation flourishes in companies where territories overlap and people have contact across functions; information flows freely; numbers of people have excesses in their budgets; many managers are in open-ended positions; and reward systems look to the future, not the past.

Ms. Kanter is professor of sociology and of organization and management at Yale University. She is also chairman of the board of Goodmeasure, Inc., a management consulting firm in Cambridge, Massachusetts. She is author of the prize-winning book, Men and Women of the Corporation *(Basic Books, 1977) and numerous other books and articles. This is her second article for HBR; the first was "Power Failures in Management Circuits," which appeared in our July-August 1979 issue and was an HBR McKinsey Award winner for that year. This article is based on research for her new book,* The Change Masters: Innovation for Productivity in the American Mode, *which Simon & Schuster will publish in February 1983.*

☐ When Steve Talbot, an operations manager, began a staff job reporting to the general manager of a product group, he had no line responsibility, no subordinates or budget of his own, and only a vague mandate to "explore options to improve performance."

To do this, Talbot set about collecting resources by bargaining with product-line managers and sales managers. By promising the product-line managers that he would save them having to negotiate with sales to get top priority for their products, he got a budget from them. Then, because he had the money in hand, Talbot got the sales managers to agree to hire one salesperson per product line, with Talbot permitted to do the hiring.

The next area he tackled was field services. Because the people in this area were conservative and tightfisted, Talbot went to his boss to get support for his recommendations about this area.

With the sales and service functions increasing their market share, it was easy for Talbot to get the product-line managers' backing when he pushed for selling a major new product that he had devised. And, to keep his action team functioning and behind him, Talbot made sure that "everyone became a hero" when the senior vice president of engineering asked him to explain his success to corporate officers.

☐ Arthur Drumm, a technical department head of two sections, wanted to develop a new measuring instrument that could dramatically improve the company's product quality. But only Drumm thought

Author's note: I'd like to thank the members of the research team who participated in this study: Karen Belinky, Janis Bowersox, Allan Cohen, Ken Farbstein, Henry Foley, William Fonvielle, Karen Handmaker, Irene Schneller, Barry Stein, David Summers, and Mary Vogel. Ken Farbstein and David Summers made especially important contributions. All individual and company names in the article are pseudonyms.

this approach would work; those around him were not convinced it was needed or would pay off. After spending months developing data to show that the company needed the instrument, Drumm convinced several of his bosses two levels up to contribute $300,000 to its development. He put together a task force made up of representatives from all the manufacturing sites to advise on the development process and to ensure that the instrument would fit in with operations.

When, early on, one high-level manager opposed the project, Drumm coached two others in preparation for an officer-level meeting at which they were going to present his proposal. And when executives argued about which budget line the money would come from, R&D or engineering, Drumm tried to ease the tension. His persistence netted the company an extremely valuable new technique.

☐   When Doris Randall became the head of a backwater purchasing department, one of three departments in her area, she expected the assignment to advance her career. Understandably, she was disappointed at the poor state of the function she had inherited and looked around for ways to make improvements. She first sought information from users of the department's services and, with this information, got her boss to agree to a first wave of changes. No one in her position had ever had such close contacts with users before, and Randall employed her knowledge to reorganize the unit into a cluster of user-oriented specialties (with each staff member concentrating on a particular need).

Once she had the reorganization in place and her function acknowledged as the best purchasing department in the region, Randall wanted to reorganize the other two purchasing departments. Her boss, perhaps out of concern that he would lose his position to Randall if the proposed changes took place, discouraged her. But her credibility was so strong that her boss's boss—who viewed her changes as a model for improvements in other areas—gave Randall the go-ahead to merge the three purchasing departments into one. Greater efficiency, cost savings, and increased user satisfaction resulted.

These three managers are enterprising, innovative, and entrepreneurial middle managers who are part of a group that can play a key role in the United States' return to economic leadership.

If that seems like an overly grand statement, consider the basis for U.S. companies' success in the past: innovation in products and advances in management techniques. Then consider the pivotal contribution middle managers make to innovation and change in large organizations. Top leaders' general directives to open a new market, improve quality, or cut costs mean nothing without efficient middle man-

agers just below officer level able to design the systems, carry them out, and redirect their staffs' activities accordingly. Furthermore, because middle managers have their fingers on the pulse of operations, they can also conceive, suggest, and set in motion new ideas that top managers may not have thought of.

The middle managers described here are not extraordinary individuals. They do, however, share a number of characteristics:

Comfort with change. They are confident that uncertainties will be clarified. They also have foresight and see unmet needs as opportunities.

Clarity of direction. They select projects carefully and, with their long time horizons, view setbacks as temporary blips in an otherwise straight path to a goal.

Thoroughness. They prepare well for meetings and are professional in making their presentations. They have insight into organizational politics and a sense of whose support can help them at various junctures.

Participative management style. They encourage subordinates to put in maximum effort and to be part of the team, promise them a share of the rewards, and deliver on their promises.

Persuasiveness, persistence, and discretion. They understand that they cannot achieve their ends overnight, so they persevere—using tact—until they do.

What makes it possible for managers to use such skills for the company's benefit? They work in organizations where the culture fosters collaboration and teamwork and where structures encourage people to "do what needs to be done." Moreover, they usually work under top managers who consciously incorporate conditions facilitating innovation and achievement into their companies' structures and operations.

These conclusions come from a study of the major accomplishments of 165 effective middle managers in five leading American corporations (for details on the research, see the ruled insert on page 118). I undertook this study to determine managers' contributions to a company's overall success as well as the conditions that stimulate innovation and thus push a business beyond a short-term emphasis and allow it to secure a successful future.

Each of the 165 managers studied—all of whom were deemed "effective" by their companies—told the research team about a particular accomplishment; these covered a wide range. Some of the successes, though impressive, clearly were achieved within the boundaries of established company practice. Others, however, involved innovation: introduction of new methods, structures, or products that

The research project

After a pilot study in which it inter-interviewed 26 effective middle managers from 18 companies, the research team interviewed, in depth, 165 middle managers from five major corporations located across the United States. The 165 were chosen by their companies to participate because of their reputations for effectiveness. We did not want a random sample: we were looking for "the best and the brightest" who could serve as models for others. It turned out, however, that every major function was represented, and roughly in proportion to its importance in the company's success. (For example, there were more innovative sales and marketing managers representing the "market-driven" company and more technical, R&D, and manufacturing managers from the "product-driven" companies.)

During the two-hour interviews, the managers talked about all aspects of a single significant accomplishment, from the glimmering of an idea to the results. We asked the managers to focus on the most significant of a set of four or five of their accomplishments over the previous two years. We also elicited a chronology of the project as well as responses to a set of open-ended questions about the acquisition of power, the handling of roadblocks, and the doling out of rewards. We supplemented the interviews with discussions about current issues in the five companies with our contacts in each company.

The five companies represent a range of types and industries: from rather traditional, slow-moving, mature companies to fast-changing, newer, high-technology companies. We included both service and manufacturing companies that are from different parts of the country and are at different stages in their development. The one thing that all five have in common is an intense interest in the topic of the study. Facing highly competitive markets (for the manufacturing companies a constant since their founding; for the service companies a newer phenomenon), all of these corporations wanted to encourage their middle managers to be more enterprising and innovative.

Our pseudonyms for the companies emphasize a central feature of each:

CHIPCO:
manufacturer of computer products

FINCO:
insurance and related financial services

MEDCO:
manufacturer of large medical equipment

RADCO (for "R&D"):
manufacturer of optical products

UTICO:
communications utility

---

increased the company's capacity. All in all, 99 of the 165 accomplishments fall within the definition of an innovative effort.

Basic accomplishments differ from innovative ones not only in scope and long-run impact but also in what it takes to achieve them. They are part of the assigned job and require only routine and readily available means to carry them out. Managers reporting this kind of accomplishment said they were just doing their jobs. Little was problematic—they had an assignment to tackle; they were told, or they already knew, how to go about it; they used existing budget or staff; they didn't need to gather or share much information outside of their units; and they encountered little or no opposition. Managers performing such activities don't generate innovations for their companies; they

merely accomplish things faster or better that they already know how to do.

In contrast, innovative accomplishments are strikingly entrepreneurial. Moreover, they are sometimes highly problematic and generally involve acquiring and using power and influence. (See the ruled insert on page 127 for more details on the study's definitions of *basic* and *innovative* accomplishments.)

In this article, I first explore how managers influence their organizations to achieve goals throughout the various stages of a project's life. Next I discuss the managerial styles of the persons studied and the kinds of innovation they brought about. I look finally at the types of companies these entrepreneurial managers worked in and explore what top officers can do to foster a creative environment.

The role of power in enterprise

Because most innovative achievements cut across organizational lines and threaten to disrupt existing arrangements, enterprising managers need tools beyond those that come with the job. Innovations have implications for other functions and areas, and they require data, agreements, and resources of wider scope than routine operations demand. Even R&D managers, who are expected to produce innovations, need more information, support, and resources for major projects than those built into regular R&D functions. They too may need additional data, more money, or agreement from extrafunctional officials that the project is necessary. Only hindsight shows that an innovative project was bound to be successful.

Because of the extra resources they require, entrepreneurial managers need to go beyond the limits of their formal positions. For this, they need power. In large organizations at least, I have observed that powerlessness "corrupts."[1] That is, lack of power (the capacity to mobilize resources and people to get things done) tends to create managers who are more concerned about guarding their territories than about collaborating with others to benefit the organization. At the same time, when managers hoard potential power and don't invest it in productive action, it atrophies and eventually blocks achievements.

Furthermore, when some people have too much unused power and others too little, problems occur. To produce results, power—like money—needs to circulate. To come up with innovations, managers have to be in areas where power circulates, where it can be grabbed and invested. In this sense, organiza-

---

1 See my book
Men and Women of the Corporation
(New York: Basic Books, 1977);
also see my article,

"Power Failure in Management Circuits,"
HBR July-August 1979, p. 65.

tional power is transactional: it exists as potential until someone makes a bid for it, invests it, and produces results with it.

The overarching condition required for managers to produce innovative achievements is this: they must envision an accomplishment beyond the scope of the job. They cannot alone possess the power to carry their idea out but they must be able to acquire the power they need easily. Thus, creative managers are not empowered simply by a boss or their job; on their own they seek and find the additional strength it takes to carry out major new initiatives. They are the corporate entrepreneurs.

Three commodities are necessary for accumulating productive power—information, resources, and support. Managers might find a portion of these within their purview and pour them into a project; managers with something they believe in will eagerly leverage their own staff and budget and even bootleg resources from their subordinates' budgets. But innovations usually require a manager to search for additional supplies elsewhere in the organization. Depending on how easy the organization makes it to tap sources of power and on how technical the project is, acquiring power can be the most time-consuming and difficult part of the process.

Phases of the accomplishment

A prototypical innovation goes through three phases: project definition (acquisition and application of information to shape a manageable, salable project), coalition building (development of a network of backers who agree to provide resources and support), and action (application of the resources, information, and support to the project and mobilization of an action team). Let us examine each of these steps in more detail.

Defining the project. Before defining a project, managers need to identify the problem. People in an organization may hold many conflicting views about the best method of reaching a goal, and discovering the basis of these conflicting perspectives (while gathering hard data) is critical to a manager's success.

In one case, information circulating freely about the original design of a part was inaccurate. The manager needed to acquire new data to prove that the problem he was about to tackle was not a manufacturing shortcoming but a design flaw. But, as often happens, some people had a stake in the popular view. Even hard-nosed engineers in our study acknowledged that, in the early stages of an entrepreneurial project, managers need political information as much as they do technical data. Without political

savvy, say these engineers, no one can get a project beyond the proposal stage.

The culmination of the project definition phase comes when managers sift through the fragments of information from each source and focus on a particular target. Then, despite the fact that managers may initially have been handed a certain area as an assignment, they still have to "sell" the project that evolves. In the innovative efforts I observed, the managers' assignments involved no promises of resources or support required to do anything more than routine activities.

Furthermore, to implement the innovation, a manager has to call on the cooperation of many others besides the boss who assigned the task. Many of these others may be independent actors who are not compelled to cooperate simply because the manager has carved a project out of a general assignment. Even subordinates may not be automatically on board. If they are professionals or managers, they have a number of other tasks and the right to set some of their own priorities; and if they are in a matrix, they may be responsible to other bosses as well.

For example, in her new job as head of a manufacturing planning unit, Heidi Wilson's assignment was to improve the cost efficiency of operations and thereby boost the company's price competitiveness. Her boss told her she could spend six months "saying nothing and just observing, getting to know what's really going on." One of the first things she noticed was that the flow of goods through the company was organized in an overly complicated, time-consuming, and expensive fashion.

The assignment gave Wilson the mandate to seek information but not to carry out any particular activities. Wilson set about to gather organizational, technical, and political information in order to translate her ambiguous task into a concrete project. She followed goods through the company to determine what the process was and how it could be changed. She sought ideas and impressions from manufacturing line managers, at the same time learning the location of vested interests and where other patches of organizational quicksand lurked. She compiled data, refined her approach, and packaged and repackaged her ideas until she believed she could "prove to people that I knew more about the company than they did."

Wilson's next step was "to do a number of punchy presentations with pictures and graphs and charts." At the presentations, she got two kinds of response: "Gee, we thought there was a problem but we never saw it outlined like this before" and "Aren't there better things to worry about?" To handle the critics, she "simply came back over and over again with information, more information than anyone else had." When she had gathered the data and received the feed-

What is an innovative accomplishment?

We categorized the 165 managers' accomplishments according to their primary impact on the company. Many accomplishments had multiple results or multiple components, but it was the breadth of scope of the accomplishment and its future utility for the company that defined its category. Immediate dollar results were *not* the central issue; rather, organizational "learning" or increased future capacity was the key. Thus, improving revenues by cutting costs while changing nothing else would be categorized differently from improving revenues by designing a new production method; only the latter leaves a lasting trace.

The accomplishments fall into two clusters:

Basic. Done solely within the existing framework and not affecting the company's longer-term capacity; 66 of the 165 fall into this category.

Innovative. A new way for the company to use or expand its resources that raises long-term capacity; 99 of the 165 are such achievements.

Basic accomplishments include:

Doing the basic job – simply carrying out adequately a defined assignment within the bounds of one's job (e.g., "fulfilled sales objectives during a reorganization").

Affecting individuals' performance – having an impact on individuals (e.g., "found employee a job in original department after failing to retrain him").

Advancing incrementally – achieving a higher level of performance within the basic job (e.g., "met more production schedules in plant than in past").

Innovative accomplishments include:

Effecting a new policy – creating a change of orientation or direction (e.g., "changed price-setting policy in product line with new model showing cost-quality trade-offs").

Finding a new opportunity – developing an entirely new product or opening a new market (e.g., "sold new product program to higher management and developed staffing for it").

Devising a fresh method – introducing a new process, procedure, or technology for continued use (e.g., "designed and implemented new information system for financial results by business sectors").

Designing a new structure – changing the formal structure, reorganizing or introducing a new structure, or forging a different link among units (e.g., "consolidated three offices into one").

While members of the research team occasionally argued about the placement of accomplishments in the subcategories, we were almost unanimous as to whether an accomplishment rated as basic or innovative. Even bringing off a financially significant or flashy increase in performance was considered basic if the accomplishment was well within the manager's assignment and territory, involved no new methods that could be used to repeat the feat elsewhere, opened no opportunities, or had no impact on corporate structure – in other words, reflected little inventiveness. The manager who achieved such a result might have been an excellent manager, but he or she was not an innovative one.

back, Wilson was ready to formulate a project and sell it to her boss. Ultimately, her project was approved, and it netted impressive cost savings.

Thus although innovation may begin with an assignment, it is usually one – like Wilson's – that is couched in general statements of results with the means largely unspecified. Occasionally, managers initiate projects themselves; however, initiation seldom occurs in a vacuum. Creative managers listen to a stream of information from superiors and peers and then identify a perceived need. In the early stages of defining a project, managers may spend more time talking with people outside their own functions than with subordinates or bosses inside.

One R&D manager said he had "hung out" with product designers while trying to get a handle on the best way to formulate a new process-development project. Another R&D manager in our survey got the idea for a new production method from a conversation about problems he had with the head of production. He then convinced his boss to let him determine whether a corrective project could be developed.

Building a coalition. Next, entrepreneurial managers need to pull in the resources and support to make the project work. For creative accomplishments, these power-related tools do not come through the vertical chain of command but rather from many areas of the organization.

George Putnam's innovation is typical. Putnam was an assistant department manager for product testing in a company that was about to demonstrate a product at a site that attracted a large number of potential buyers. Putnam heard through the grapevine that a decision was imminent about which model to display. The product managers were each lobbying for their own, and the marketing people also had a favorite. Putnam, who was close to the products, thought that the first-choice model had grave defects and so decided to demonstrate to the marketing staff both what the problems with the first one were and the superiority of another model.

Building on a long-term relationship with the people in corporate quality control and a good alliance with his boss, Putnam sought the tools he needed: the blessing of the vice president of engineering (his boss's boss), special materials for testing from the materials division, a budget from corporate quality control, and staff from his own units to carry out the tests. As Putnam put it, this was all done through one-on-one "horse trading" – showing each manager how much the others were chipping in. Then Putnam met informally with the key marketing staffer to learn what it would take to convince him.

As the test results emerged, Putnam took them to his peers in marketing, engineering, and quality control so they could feed them to their superiors. The accumulated support persuaded the decision makers to adopt Putnam's choice of a model; it later became a strong money-maker. In sum, Putnam had completely stepped out of his usual role to build a consensus that shaped a major policy decision.

Thus the most successful innovations derive from situations where a number of people from a number of areas make contributions. They provide a kind of checks-and-balances system to an activity that is otherwise nonroutine and, therefore, is not subject to the usual controls. By building a coalition before extensive project activity gets under way, the manager also ensures the availability of enough support to keep momentum going and to guarantee implementation.

In one company, the process of lining up peers and stakeholders as early supporters is called "making cheerleaders"; in another, "preselling." Sometimes managers ask peers for "pledges" of money or staff to be collected later if higher management approves the project and provides overall resources.

After garnering peer support, usually managers next seek support at much higher levels. While we found surprisingly few instances of top management directly sponsoring or championing a project, we did find that a general blessing from the top is clearly necessary to convert potential supporters into a solid team. In one case, top officers simply showed up at a meeting where the proposal was being discussed; their presence ensured that other people couldn't use the "pocket veto" power of headquarters as an excuse to table the issue. Also, the very presence of a key executive at such a meeting is often a signal of the proposal's importance to the rest of the organization.

Enterprising managers learn who at the top-executive level has the power to affect their projects (including material resources or vital initial approval power). Then they negotiate for these executives' support, using polished formal presentations. Whereas managers can often sell the project to peers and stakeholders by appealing to these people's self-interests and assuring them they know what they're talking about, managers need to offer top executives more guarantees about both the technical and the political adequacies of projects.

Key executives tend to evaluate a proposal in terms of its salability to *their* constituencies. Sometimes entrepreneurial managers arm top executives with materials or rehearse them for their own presentations to other people (such as members of an executive committee or the board) who have to approve the project.

Most often, since many of the projects that originate at the middle of a company can be supported at that level and will not tap corporate funds, those at high levels in the organization simply provide a general expression of support. However, the attention top management confers on this activity, many of our interviewees told us, makes it possible to sell their own staffs as well as others.

But once in a while, a presentation to top-level officers results in help in obtaining supplies. Sometimes enterprising managers walk away with the promise of a large capital expenditure or assistance getting staff or space. Sometimes a promise of resources is contingent on getting others on board. "If you can raise the money, go ahead with this," is a frequent directive to an enterprising manager.

In one situation, a service manager approached his boss and his boss's boss for a budget for a college recruitment and training program that he had been supporting on his own with funds bootlegged from his staff. The top executives told him they would grant a large budget if he could get his four peers to support the project. Somewhat to their surprise, he came back with this support. He had taken his peers away from the office for three days for a round of negotiation and planning. In cases like this, top management is not so much hedging its bets as using its ability to secure peer support for what might otherwise be risky projects.

With promises of resources and support in hand, enterprising managers can go back to the immediate boss or bosses to make plans for moving ahead. Usually the bosses are simply waiting for this tangible sign of power to continue authorizing the project. But in other cases the bosses are not fully involved and won't be sold until the manager has higher-level support.

Of course, during the coalition-building phase, the network of supporters does not play a passive role; their comments, criticisms, and objectives help shape the project into one that is more likely to succeed. Another result of the coalition-building phase is, then, a set of reality checks that ensures that projects unlikely to succeed will go no farther.

Moving into action. The innovating manager's next step is to mobilize key players to carry out the project. Whether the players are nominal subordinates or a special project group such as a task force, managers forge them into a team. Enterprising managers bring the people involved in the project together, give them briefings and assignments, pump them up for the extra effort needed, seek their ideas and suggestions (both as a way to involve them and to further refine the project), and promise them a share of the rewards. As one manager put it, "It takes more selling than telling." In most of the innovations we observed, the manager couldn't just order subordinates to get involved. Doing something beyond routine work that involves creativity and cooperation requires the full commitment of subordinates; otherwise the project will not succeed.

During the action phase, managers have four central organizational tasks. The technical details of the project and the actual work directed toward project goals are now in the hands of the action team. Managers may contribute ideas or even get involved in hands-on experimentation, but their primary functions are still largely external and organizational, centered around maintaining the boundaries and integrity of the project.

The manager's first task is to **handle interference** or opposition that may jeopardize the project. Entrepreneurial managers encounter strikingly little overt opposition—perhaps because their success at coalition building determines whether a project gets started in the first place. Resistance takes a more passive form: criticism of the plan's details, foot-dragging, late responses to requests, or arguments over allocation of time and resources among projects.

Managers are sometimes surprised that critics keep so quiet up to this point. One manufacturing manager who was gearing up for production of a new item had approached many executives in other areas while making cost estimates, and these executives had appeared positive about his efforts. But later, when he began organizing the manufacturing process itself, he heard objections from these very people.

During this phase, therefore, innovative managers may have to spend as much time in meetings, both formal and one-to-one, as they did to get the project launched. Managers need to prepare thoroughly for these meetings so they can counter skepticism and objections with clear facts, persuasion, and reminders of the benefits that can accrue to managers meeting the project's objectives. In most cases, a clear presentation of facts is enough. But not always: one of our respondents, a high-level champion, had to tell an opponent to back down, that the project was going ahead anyway, and that his carping was annoying.

Whereas managers need to directly counter open challenges and criticism that might result in the flow of power or supplies being cut off, they simply keep other interference outside the boundaries of the project. In effect, the manager defines a protected area for the group's work. He or she goes outside this area to head off critics and to keep people or rules imposed by higher management from disrupting project tasks.

While the team itself is sometimes unaware of the manager's contribution, the manager—like Tom West (head of the now-famous computer-design group at Data General)—patrols the boundaries.[2] Acting as interference filters, managers in my study protected innovative projects by bending

2 Tracy Kidder,
The Soul of a New Machine
(Boston: Little, Brown, 1981).

rules, transferring funds "illicitly" from one budget line to another, developing special reward or incentive systems that offered bonuses above company pay rates, and ensuring that superiors stayed away unless needed.

The second action-phase task is **maintaining momentum** and continuity. Here interference comes from internal rather than external sources. Foot-dragging or inactivity is a constant danger, especially if the creative effort adds to work loads. In our study, enterprising managers as well as team members complained continually about the tendency for routine activities to take precedence over special projects and to consume limited time.

In addition, it is easier for managers to whip up excitement over a vision at start-up than to keep the goal in people's minds when they face the tedium of the work. Thus, managers' team-building skills are essential. So the project doesn't lose momentum, managers must sustain the enthusiasm of all—from supporters to suppliers—by being persistent and keeping the team aware of supportive authorities who are clearly waiting for results.

One manager, who was involved in a full-time project to develop new and more efficient methods of producing a certain ingredient, maintained momentum by holding daily meetings with the core team, getting together often with operations managers and members of a task force he had formed, putting out weekly status reports, and making frequent presentations to top management. When foot-dragging occurs, many entrepreneurial managers pull in high-level supporters—without compromising the autonomy of the project—to get the team back on board. A letter or a visit from the big boss can remind everyone just how important the project is.

A third task of middle managers in the action phase is to engage in whatever **secondary redesign**—other changes made to support the key change—is necessary to keep the project going. For example, a manager whose team was setting up a computerized information bank held weekly team meetings to define tactics. A fallout of these meetings was a set of new awards and a fresh performance appraisal system for team members and their subordinates.

As necessary, managers introduce new arrangements to conjoin with the core tasks. When it seems that a project is bogging down—that is, when everything possible has been done and no more results are on the horizon—managers often change the structure or approach. Such alterations can cause a redoubling of effort and a renewed attack on the problem. They can also bring the company additional unplanned innovations as a side benefit from the main project.

The fourth task of the action phase, **external communication,** brings the accomplishment full circle. The project begins with gathering information; now it is important to send information out. It is vital to (as several managers put it) "manage the press" so that peers and key supporters have an up-to-date impression of the project and its success. Delivering on promises is also important. As much as possible, innovative managers meet deadlines, deliver early benefits to others, and keep supporters supplied with information. Doing so establishes the credibility of both the project and the manager, even before concrete results can be shown.

Information must be shared with the team and the coalition as well. Good managers periodically remind the team of what they stand to gain from the accomplishment, hold meetings to give feedback and to stimulate pride in the project, and make a point of congratulating each staff member individually. After all, as Steve Talbot (of my first example) said, many people gave this middle manager power because of a promise that everyone would be a hero.

assigned, they don't need external support; because they have all the tools to do it, they don't need to get anyone else involved (they simply direct subordinates to do what is required). But for innovative accomplishments—seeking funds, staff, or information (political as well as technical) from outside the work unit; attending long meetings and presentations; and requiring "above and beyond" effort from staff—a style that revolves around participation, collaboration, and persuasion is essential.

The participative-collaborative style also helps creative managers reduce risk because it encourages completion of the assignment. Furthermore, others' involvement serves as a check-and-balance on the project, reshaping it to make it more of a sure thing and putting pressure on people to follow through. The few projects in my study that disintegrated did so because the manager failed to build a coalition of supporters and collaborators.

A management style for innovation...

Clearly there is a strong association between carrying out an innovative accomplishment and employing a participative-collaborative management style. The managers observed reached success by:

Persuading more than ordering, though managers sometimes use pressure as a last resort.

Building a team, which entails among other things frequent staff meetings and considerable sharing of information.

Seeking inputs from others—that is, asking for ideas about users' needs, soliciting suggestions from subordinates, welcoming peer review, and so forth.

Acknowledging others' stake or potential stake in the project—in other words, being politically sensitive.

Sharing rewards and recognition willingly.

A collaborative style is also useful when carrying out basic accomplishments; however, in such endeavors it is not required. Managers can bring off many basic accomplishments using a traditional, more autocratic style. Because they're doing what is

...and corporate conditions that encourage enterprise

Just as the manager's strategies to develop and implement innovations followed many different patterns, so also the level of enterprise managers achieved varied strongly across the five companies we studied (see the *Exhibit*). Managers in newer, high-technology companies have a much higher proportion of innovative accomplishments than managers in other industries. At "CHIPCO," a computer parts manufacturer, 71% of all the things effective managers did were innovative; for "UTICO," a communications utility, the number is 33%; for "FINCO," an insurance company, it is 47%.

This difference in levels of innovative achievement correlates with the extent to which these companies' structures and cultures support middle managers' creativity. Companies producing the most entrepreneurs have cultures that encourage collaboration and teamwork. Moreover, they have complex structures that link people in multiple ways and help them go beyond the confines of their defined jobs to do "what needs to be done."

CHIPCO, which showed the most entrepreneurial activity of any company in our study, is a rapidly growing electronics company with abundant resources. That its culture favors independent action and team effort is communicated quickly and clearly to the newcomer. Sources of support and money are constantly shifting and, as growth occurs, managers rapidly move on to other positions. But even though people frequently express frustration about the

Exhibit	Characteristics of the five companies in order of most to least "entrepreneurial"				
	CHIPCO	**RADCO**	**MEDCO**	**FINCO**	**UTICO**
Percent of effective managers with entrepreneurial accomplishments	71 %	69 %	67 %	47 %	33 %
Current economic trend	Steadily up	Trend up but currently down	Up	Mixed	Down
Current "change issues"	Change "normal"; constant change in product generations; proliferating staff and units.	Change "normal" in products, technologies; recent changeover to second management generation with new focus.	Reorganized about 3-4 years ago to install matrix; "normal" product technology changes.	Change a "shock"; new top management group from outside reorganizing and trying to add competitive market posture.	Change a "shock"; undergoing reorganization to install matrix and add competitive market posture while reducing staff.
Organization structure	Matrix	Matrix in some areas; product lines act as quasi-divisions.	Matrix in some areas.	Divisional; unitary hierarchy within divisions, some central services.	Functional organization; currently overlaying a matrix of regions and markets.
	Decentralized	Mixed	Mixed	Centralized	Centralized
Information flow	Free	Free	Moderately free	Constricted	Constricted
Communication emphasis	Horizontal	Horizontal	Horizontal	Vertical	Vertical
Culture	Clear, consistent; favors individual initiative.	Clear, though in transition from emphasis on invention to emphasis on routinization and systems.	Clear; pride in company, belief that talent will be rewarded.	Idiosyncratic; depends on boss and area.	Clear but top management would like to change it; favors security, maintenance, protection.
Current "emotional" climate	Pride in company, team feeling, some "burn-out."	Uncertainty about changes.	Pride in company, team feeling.	Low trust, high uncertainty.	High certainty, confusion.
Rewards	Abundant. Include visibility, chance to do more challenging work in the future and get bigger budget for projects.	Abundant. Include visibility, chance to do more challenging work in future and get bigger budget for projects.	Moderately abundant. Conventional.	Scarce. Primarily monetary.	Scarce. Promotion, salary freeze; recognition by peers grudging.

shifting approval process, slippage of schedules, and continual entry of new players onto the stage, they don't complain about lost opportunities. For one thing, because coalitions support the various projects, new project managers feel bound to honor their predecessors' financial commitments.

CHIPCO managers have broad job charters to "do the right thing" in a manner of their own choosing. Lateral relationships are more important than vertical ones. Most functions are in a matrix, and some managers have up to four "bosses." Top management expects ideas to bubble up from lower levels. Senior executives then select solutions rather than issue confining directives. In fact, people generally rely on informal face-to-face communication across units to build a consensus. Managers spend a lot of time in meetings; information flows freely, and reputation among peers—instead of formal authority or title—conveys credibility and garners support. Career mobility at CHIPCO is rapid, and people have pride in the company's success.

RADCO, the company with the strongest R&D orientation in the study, has many of

CHIPCO's qualities but bears the burden of recent changes. RADCO's once-strong culture and its image as a research institute are in flux and may be eroding. A new top management with new ways of thinking is shifting the orientation of the company, and some people express concern about the lack of clear direction and long-range planning. People's faith in RADCO's strategy of technical superiority has weakened, and its traditional orientation toward innovation is giving way to a concern for routinization and production efficiency. This shift is resulting in conflict and uncertainty. Where once access to the top was easy, now the decentralized matrix structure—with fewer central services—makes it difficult.

As at CHIPCO, lateral relationships are important, though top management's presence is felt more. In the partial matrix, some managers have as many as four "bosses." A middle manager's boss or someone in higher management is likely to give general support to projects as long as peers (within and across functions) get on board. And peers often work decisions up the organization through their own hierarchies.

Procedures at RADCO are both informal and formal: much happens at meetings and presentations and through persuasion, plus the company's long-term employment and well-established working relationships encourage lateral communication. But managers also use task forces and steering committees. Projects often last for years, sustained by the company's image as a leader in treating employees well.

MEDCO manufactures and sells advanced medical equipment, often applying ideas developed elsewhere. Although MEDCO produces a high proportion of innovative accomplishments, it has a greater degree of central planning and routinization than either CHIPCO or RADCO. Despite headquarters' strong role, heads of functions and product managers can vary their approaches. Employers believe that MEDCO's complex matrix system allows autonomy and creates opportunities but is also time wasting because clear accountability is lacking.

Teamwork and competition coexist at MEDCO. Although top management officially encourages teamwork and the matrix produces a tendency for trades and selling to go on within the organization, interdepartmental and interproduct rivalries sometimes get in the way. Rewards, especially promotions, are available, but they often come late and even then are not always clear or consistent. Because many employees have been with MEDCO for a long time, both job mobility and job security are high. Finally, managers see the company as a leader in its approach to management and as a technological follower in all areas but one.

The last two companies in the study, FINCO (insurance) and UTICO (communications), show the lowest proportion of innovative achievements. Many of the completed projects seemed to be successful *despite* the system.

Currently FINCO has an idiosyncratic and inconsistent culture: employees don't have a clear image of the company, its style, or its direction. How managers are treated depends very much on one's boss—one-to-one relationships and private deals carry a great deal of weight. Though the atmosphere of uncertainty creates opportunities for a few, it generally limits risk taking. Moreover, reorganizations, a top-management shake-up, and shuffling of personnel have fostered insecurity and suspicion. It is difficult for managers to get commitment from their subordinates because they question the manager's tenure. Managers spend much time and energy coping with change, reassuring subordinates, and orienting new staff instead of developing future-oriented projects. Still, because the uncertainty creates a vacuum, a few managers in powerful positions (many of whom were brought in to initiate change) do benefit.

Unlike the innovation-producing companies, FINCO features vertical relationships. With little encouragement to collaborate, managers seldom make contact across functions or work in teams. Managers often see formal structures and systems as constraints rather than as supports. Rewards are scarce, and occasionally a manager will break a promise about them. Seeing the company as a follower, not a leader, the managers at FINCO sometimes make unfavorable comparisons between it and other companies in the industry. Furthermore, they resent the fact that FINCO's top management brings in so many executives from outside; they see it as an insult.

UTICO is a very good company in many ways; it is well regarded by its employees and is considered progressive for its industry. However, despite the strong need for UTICO to be more creative and thus more competitive and despite movement toward a matrix structure, UTICO's middle ranks aren't very innovative. UTICO's culture is changing—from being based on security and maintenance to being based on flexibility and competition—and the atmosphere of uncertainty frustrates achievers. Moreover, UTICO remains very centralized. Top management largely directs searches for new systems and methods through formal mechanisms whose ponderousness sometimes discourages innovation. Tight budgetary constraints make it difficult for middle managers to tap funds; carefully measured duties discourage risk takers; and a lockstep chain of command makes it dangerous for managers to bypass their bosses.

Information flows vertically and sluggishly. Because of limited cooperation among work units, even technical data can be hard to get. Weak-spot management means that problems, not successes, get attention. Jealousy and competition over turf kill praise from peers and sometimes from bosses. Managers' image of the company is mixed: they see it as leading its type of business but behind more modern companies in rate of change.

Organizational supports for creativity

Examination of the differences in organization, culture, and practices in these five companies makes clear the circumstances under which enterprise can flourish. To tackle and solve tricky problems, people need both the opportunities and the incentives to reach beyond their formal jobs and combine organizational resources in new ways.[3] The following create these opportunities:

☐   Multiple reporting relationships and overlapping territories. These force middle managers to carve out their own ideas about appropriate action and to sell peers in neighboring areas or more than one boss.

☐ A free and somewhat random flow of information. Data flow of this kind prods executives to find ideas in unexpected places and pushes them to combine fragments of information.

☐ Many centers of power with some budgetary flexibility. If such centers are easily accessible to middle managers, they will be encouraged to make proposals and acquire resources.

☐ A high proportion of managers in loosely defined positions or with ambiguous assignments. Those without subordinates or line responsibilities who are told to "solve problems" must argue for a budget or develop their own constituency.

☐ Frequent and smooth cross-functional contact, a tradition of working in teams and sharing credit widely, and emphasis on lateral rather than vertical relationships as a source of resources, information, and support. These circumstances require managers to get peer support for their projects before top officers approve.

☐ A reward system that emphasizes investment in people and projects rather than payment for past services. Such a system encourages executives to move into challenging jobs, gives them budgets to tackle projects, and rewards them after their accomplishments with the chance to take on even bigger projects in the future.

Some of these conditions seem to go hand in hand with new companies in not-yet-mature markets. But top decision makers in older, traditional companies can design these conditions into their organizations. They would be wise to do so because, if empowered, innovative middle managers can be one of America's most potent weapons in its battle against foreign competition. ▽

Reprint 82407

Building a team

There was, it appeared, a mysterious rite of initiation through which, in one way or another, almost every member of the team passed. The term that the old hands used for this rite — West invented the term, not the practice — was "signing up." By signing up for the project you agreed to do whatever was necessary for success. You agreed to forsake, if necessary, family, hobbies, and friends — if you had any of these left (and you might not if you had signed up too many times before). From a manager's point of view, the practical virtues of the ritual were manifold. Labor was no longer coerced. Labor volunteered. When you signed up you in effect declared, "I want to do this job and I'll give it my heart and soul." It cut another way. The vice president of engineering, Carl Carman, who knew the term, said much later on: "Sometimes I worry that I pushed too hard. I tried not to push any harder than I would on myself. That's why, by the way, you have to go through the sign-up. To be sure you're not conning anybody."

The rite was not accomplished with formal declarations, as a rule. Among the old hands, a statement such as "Yeah, I'll do that" could constitute the act of signing up, and often it was done tacitly — as when, without being ordered to do so, Alsing took on the role of chief recruiter.

The old hands knew the game and what they were getting into. The new recruits, however, presented some problems in this regard.

From
The Soul of a New Machine
by Tracy Kidder.
Boston: Little, Brown and Company, 1981.
Reprinted with permission from the publisher.

3 My findings about conditions stimulating managerial innovations are generally consistent with those on technical (R&D) innovation. See James Utterback, "Innovation in Industry," *Science* February 1974, pp. 620-626; John Kimberly, "Managerial Innovation," *Handbook of Organizational Design*, edited by W.H. Starbuck (New York: Oxford, 1981); and Goodmeasure, Inc., "99 Propositions on Innovation from the Research Literature," *Stimulating Innovation in Middle Management* (Cambridge, Mass., 1982).

Managing
Up and Down

Managing your boss

A compatible relationship with your superior is essential to being effective in your job

John J. Gabarro and John P. Kotter

Good managers recognize that a relationship with a boss involves mutual dependence and that, if it is not managed well, they cannot be effective in their jobs. They also recognize that the boss-subordinate relationship is not like the one between a parent and a child, in that the burden for managing the relationship should not and cannot fall entirely on the boss. Bosses are only human; their wisdom and maturity are not always greater than their subordinates'. Effective managers see managing the relationship with the boss as part of their job. As a result, they take time and energy to develop a relationship that is consonant with both persons' styles and assets and that meets the most critical needs of each.

Mr. Gabarro is professor of organizational behavior at the Harvard Business School. His main area of research is how executives build effective working relationships. His most recent publication is *Interpersonal Behavior* (Englewood Cliffs, N.J.: Prentice-Hall, 1978), which he coauthored with Anthony G. Athos. Mr. Kotter is associate professor of organizational behavior at the Harvard Business School. This is his third article in HBR, the most recent being "Choosing Strategies for Change," March-April 1979, coauthored by Leonard A. Schlesinger.

Drawings by Arnie Levin.

To many the phrase *managing your boss* may sound unusual or suspicious. Because of the traditional top-down emphasis in organizations, it is not obvious why you need to manage relationships upward—unless, of course, you would do so for personal or political reasons. But in using the expression *managing your boss*, we are not referring to political maneuvering or apple polishing. Rather, we are using the term to mean the process of consciously working with your superior to obtain the best possible results for you, your boss, and the company.

Recent studies suggest that effective managers take time and effort to manage not only relationships with their subordinates but also those with their bosses.[1] These studies show as well that this aspect of management, essential though it is to survival and advancement, is sometimes ignored by otherwise talented and aggressive managers. Indeed, some managers who actively and effectively supervise subordinates, products, markets, and technologies, nevertheless assume an almost passively reactive stance vis-à-vis their bosses. Such a stance practically always hurts these managers and their companies.

If you doubt the importance of managing your relationship with your boss or how difficult it is to do so effectively, consider for a moment the following sad but telling story:

Frank Gibbons was an acknowledged manufacturing genius in his industry and, by any profitability standard, a very effective executive. In 1973, his

---

1. See, for example, John J. Gabarro, "Socialization at the Top: How CEOs and Their Subordinates Develop Interpersonal Contracts," *Organizational Dynamics*, Winter 1979; and John P. Kotter, *Power in Management*, AMACOM, 1979.

strengths propelled him into the position of vice president of manufacturing for the second largest and most profitable company in its industry. Gibbons was not, however, a good manager of people. He knew this, as did others in his company and his industry. Recognizing this weakness, the president made sure that those who reported to Gibbons were good at working with people and could compensate for his limitations. The arrangement worked well.

In 1975, Philip Bonnevie was promoted into a position reporting to Gibbons. In keeping with the previous pattern, the president selected Bonnevie because he had an excellent track record and a reputation for being good with people. In making that selection, however, the president neglected to notice that, in his rapid rise through the organization, Bonnevie himself had never reported to anyone who was poor at managing subordinates. Bonnevie had always had good-to-excellent bosses. He had never been forced to manage a relationship with a difficult boss. In retrospect, Bonnevie admits he had never thought that managing his boss was a part of his job.

Fourteen months after he started working for Gibbons, Bonnevie was fired. During that same quarter, the company reported a net loss for the first time in seven years. Many of those who were close to these events say that they don't really understand what happened. This much is known, however: while the company was bringing out a major new product—a process that required its sales, engineering, and manufacturing groups to coordinate their decisions very carefully—a whole series of misunderstandings and bad feelings developed between Gibbons and Bonnevie.

For example, Bonnevie claims Gibbons was aware of and had accepted Bonnevie's decision to use a new type of machinery to make the new product; Gibbons swears he did not. Furthermore, Gibbons claims he made it clear to Bonnevie that introduction of the product was too important to the company in the short run to take any major risks.

As a result of such misunderstandings, planning went awry: a new manufacturing plant was built that could not produce the new product designed by engineering, in the volume desired by sales, at a cost agreed on by the executive committee. Gibbons blamed Bonnevie for the mistake. Bonnevie blamed Gibbons.

Of course, one could argue that the problem here was caused by Gibbons's inability to manage his subordinates. But one can make just as strong a case that the problem was related to Bonnevie's inability to manage his boss. Remember, Gibbons was

not having difficulty with any other subordinates. Moreover, given the personal price paid by Bonnevie (being fired and having his reputation within the industry severely tarnished), there was little consolation in saying the problem was that Gibbons was poor at managing subordinates. Everyone already knew that.

We believe that the situation could have turned out differently had Bonnevie been more adept at understanding Gibbons and at managing his relationship with him. In this case, an inability to manage upward was unusually costly. The company lost $2 to $5 million, and Bonnevie's career was, at least temporarily, disrupted. Many less costly cases like this probably occur regularly in all major corporations, and the cumulative effect can be very destructive.

Misreading the boss-subordinate relationship

People often dismiss stories like the one we just related as being merely cases of personality conflict. Because two people can on occasion be psychologically or temperamentally incapable of working together, this can be an apt description. But more often, we have found, a personality conflict is only a part of the problem—sometimes a very small part.

Bonnevie did not just have a different personality from Gibbons, he also made or had unrealistic assumptions and expectations about the very nature of boss-subordinate relationships. Specifically, he did not recognize that his relationship to Gibbons involved *mutual dependence* between two *fallible* human beings. Failing to recognize this, a manager typically either avoids trying to manage his or her relationship with a boss or manages it ineffectively.

Some people behave as if their bosses were not very dependent on them. They fail to see how much the boss needs their help and cooperation to do his or her job effectively. These people refuse to acknowledge that the boss can be severely hurt by their actions and needs cooperation, dependability, and honesty from them.

Some see themselves as not very dependent on their bosses. They gloss over how much help and information they need from the boss in order to perform their own jobs well. This superficial view is particularly damaging when a manager's job and decisions affect other parts of the organization, as was the case in Bonnevie's situation. A manager's immediate boss can play a critical role in linking the manager to the rest of the organization, in making sure the manager's priorities are consistent with organizational needs, and in securing the resources the manager needs to perform well. Yet some managers need to see themselves as practically self-sufficient, as not needing the critical information and resources a boss can supply.

Many managers, like Bonnevie, assume that the boss will magically know what information or help their subordinates need and provide it to them. Certainly, some bosses do an excellent job of caring for their subordinates in this way, but for a manager to expect that from all bosses is dangerously unrealistic. A more reasonable expectation for managers to have is that modest help will be forthcoming. After all, bosses are only human. Most really effective managers accept this fact and assume primary responsibility for their own careers and development. They make a point of seeking the information and help they need to do a job instead of waiting for their bosses to provide it.

In light of the foregoing, it seems to us that managing a situation of mutual dependence among fallible human beings requires the following:

> That you have a good understanding of the other person and yourself, especially regarding strengths, weaknesses, work styles, and needs.

> That you use this information to develop and manage a healthy working relationship—one which is compatible with both persons' work styles and assets, is characterized by mutual expectations, and meets the most critical needs of the other person. And that is essentially what we have found highly effective managers doing.

Understanding the boss & yourself

Managing your boss requires that you gain an understanding of both the boss and his context as well as your own situation and needs. All managers do this to some degree, but many are not thorough enough.

The boss's world

At a minimum, you need to appreciate your boss's goals and pressures, his or her strengths and weaknesses. What are your boss's organizational and personal objectives, and what are the pressures on him, especially those from his boss and others at his level? What are your boss's long suits and blind spots? What is his or her preferred style of working? Does he or she like to get information through memos, formal meetings, or phone calls? Does your boss thrive on conflict or try to minimize it?

Without this information, a manager is flying blind when dealing with his boss, and unnecessary conflicts, misunderstandings, and problems are inevitable.

Goals & pressures

In one situation we studied, a top-notch marketing manager with a superior performance record was hired into a company as a vice president "to straighten out the marketing and sales problems." The company, which was having financial difficulties, had been recently acquired by a larger corporation. The president was eager to turn it around and gave the new marketing vice president free rein—at least initially. Based on his previous experience, the new vice president correctly diagnosed that greater market share was needed and that strong product management was required to bring that about. As a result, he made a number of pricing decisions aimed at increasing high-volume business.

When margins declined and the financial situation did not improve, however, the president increased pressure on the new vice president. Believing that the situation would eventually correct itself as the company gained back market share, the vice president resisted the pressure.

When by the second quarter margins and profits had still failed to improve, the president took direct control over all pricing decisions and put all items on a set level of margin, regardless of volume. The new vice president began to find himself shut out by the president, and their relationship deteriorated. In fact, the vice president found the president's behavior bizarre. Unfortunately, the president's new pricing scheme also failed to increase margins, and by the fourth quarter both the president and the vice president were fired.

What the new vice president had not known until it was too late was that improving marketing and sales had been only *one* of the president's goals. His most immediate goal had been to make the company more profitable—quickly.

Nor had the new vice president known that his boss was invested in this short-term priority for personal as well as business reasons. The president had been a strong advocate of the acquisition with-

in the parent company, and his personal credibility was at stake.

The vice president made three basic errors. He took information supplied to him at face value, he made assumptions in areas where he had no information, and—most damaging—he never actively tried to clarify what his boss's objectives were. As a result, he ended up taking actions that were actually at odds with the president's priorities and objectives.

Managers who work effectively with their bosses do not behave this way. They seek out information about the boss's goals and problems and pressures. They are alert for opportunities to question the boss and others around him to test their assumptions. They pay attention to clues in the boss's behavior. Although it is imperative they do this when they begin working with a new boss, effective managers also do this on an ongoing basis because they recognize that priorities and concerns change.

Strengths, weaknesses & work style

Being sensitive to a boss's work style can be crucial, especially when the boss is new. For example, a new president who was organized and formal in his approach replaced a man who was informal and intuitive. The new president worked best when he had written reports. He also preferred formal meetings with set agendas.

One of his division managers realized this need and worked with the new president to identify the kinds and frequency of information and reports the president wanted. This manager also made a point of sending background information and brief agendas for their discussions. He found that with this type of preparation their meetings were very useful. Moreover, he found that with adequate preparation his new boss was even more effective at brainstorming problems than his more informal and intuitive predecessor had been.

In contrast, another division manager never fully understood how the new boss's work style differed from that of his predecessor. To the degree that he did sense it, he experienced it as too much control. As a result, he seldom sent the new president the background information he needed, and the president never felt fully prepared for meetings with the manager. In fact, the president spent much of his time when they met trying to get information that he felt he should have had before his arrival. The boss experienced these meetings as frustrating and inefficient, and the subordinate often found himself thrown off guard by the questions that the president asked. Ultimately, this division manager resigned.

The difference between the two division managers just described was not so much one of ability or even adaptability. Rather, the difference was that one of the men was more sensitive to his boss's work style than the other and to the implications of his boss's needs.

You & your needs

The boss is only one-half of the relationship. You are the other half, as well as the part over which you have more direct control. Developing an effective working relationship requires, then, that you know your own needs, strengths and weaknesses, and personal style.

Your own style

You are not going to change either your basic personality structure or that of your boss. But you can become aware of what it is about you that impedes or facilitates working with your boss and, with that awareness, take actions that make the relationship more effective.

For example, in one case we observed, a manager and his superior ran into problems whenever they disagreed. The boss's typical response was to harden his position and overstate it. The manager's reaction was then to raise the ante and intensify the forcefulness of his argument. In doing this, he channeled his anger into sharpening his attacks on the logical fallacies in his boss's assumptions. His boss in turn would become even more adamant about holding his original position. Predictably, this escalating cycle resulted in the subordinate avoiding whenever possible any topic of potential conflict with his boss.

In discussing this problem with his peers, the manager discovered that his reaction to the boss was typical of how he generally reacted to counterarguments—but with a difference. His response would overwhelm his peers, but not his boss. Because his attempts to discuss this problem with his boss were unsuccessful, he concluded that the only way to change the situation was to deal with his own instinctive reactions. Whenever the two reached an impasse, he would check his own impatience and suggest that they break up and think about it before getting together again. Usually when they renewed their discussion, they had digested their differences and were more able to work them through.

Gaining this level of self-awareness and acting on it are difficult but not impossible. For example, by reflecting over his past experiences, a young manager learned that he was not very good at dealing with difficult and emotional issues where people were involved. Because he disliked those issues and realized that his instinctive responses to them were seldom very good, he developed a habit of touching base with his boss whenever such a problem arose. Their discussions always surfaced ideas and approaches the manager had not considered. In many cases, they also identified specific actions the boss could take to help.

Dependence on authority figures

Although a superior-subordinate relationship is one of mutual dependence, it is also one in which the subordinate is typically more dependent on the boss than the other way around. This dependence inevitably results in the subordinate feeling a certain degree of frustration, sometimes anger, when his actions or options are constrained by his boss's decisions. This is a normal part of life and occurs in the best of relationships. The way in which a manager handles these frustrations largely depends on his or her predisposition toward dependence on authority figures.

Some people's instinctive reaction under these circumstances is to resent the boss's authority and to rebel against the boss's decisions. Sometimes a person will escalate a conflict beyond what is appropriate. Seeing the boss almost as an institutional enemy, this type of manager will often, without being conscious of it, fight with the boss just for the sake of fighting. His reactions to being constrained are usually strong and sometimes impulsive. He sees the boss as someone who, by virtue of his role, is a hindrance to progress, an obstacle to be circumvented or at best tolerated.

Psychologists call this pattern of reactions counterdependent behavior. Although a counterdependent person is difficult for most superiors to manage and usually has a history of strained relationships with superiors, this sort of manager is apt to have even more trouble with a boss who tends to be directive or authoritarian. When the manager acts on his or her negative feelings, often in subtle and nonverbal ways, the boss sometimes *does* become the enemy. Sensing the subordinate's latent hostility, the boss will lose trust in the subordinate or his judgment and behave less openly.

Paradoxically, a manager with this type of predisposition is often a good manager of his own people. He will often go out of his way to get support for them and will not hesitate to go to bat for them.

At the other extreme are managers who swallow their anger and behave in a very compliant fashion when the boss makes what they know to be a poor decision. These managers will agree with the boss even when a disagreement might be welcome or when the boss would easily alter his decision if given more information. Because they bear no relationship to the specific situation at hand, their responses are as much an overreaction as those of counterdependent managers. Instead of seeing the boss as an enemy, these people deny their anger—the other extreme—and tend to see the boss as if he or she were an all-wise parent who should know best, should take responsibility for their careers, train them in all they need to know, and protect them from overly ambitious peers.

Both counterdependence and overdependence lead managers to hold unrealistic views of what a boss is. Both views ignore that most bosses, like everyone else, are imperfect and fallible. They don't have unlimited time, encyclopedic knowledge, or extrasensory perception; nor are they evil enemies. They have their own pressures and concerns that are sometimes at odds with the wishes of the subordinate—and often for good reason.

Altering predispositions toward authority, especially at the extremes, is almost impossible without intensive psychotherapy (psychoanalytic theory and research suggest that such predispositions are deeply rooted in a person's personality and upbringing). However, an awareness of these extremes and the range between them can be very useful in understanding where your own predispositions fall and what the implications are for how you tend to behave in relation to your boss.

If you believe, on the one hand, that you have some tendencies toward counterdependence, you can understand and even predict what your reactions and overreactions are likely to be. If, on the other hand, you believe you have some tendencies toward overdependence, you might question the extent to which your overcompliance or inability to confront real differences may be making both you and your boss less effective.

Developing & managing the relationship

With a clear understanding of both your boss and yourself, you can—usually—establish a way of working together that fits both of you, that is characterized by unambiguous mutual expectations, and that helps both of you to be more productive and effec-

tive. We have already outlined a few things such a relationship consists of, which are itemized in the *Exhibit*, and here are a few more.

Compatible work styles

Above all else, a good working relationship with a boss accommodates differences in work style. For example, in one situation we studied, a manager (who had a relatively good relationship with his superior) realized that during meetings his boss would often become inattentive and sometimes brusque. The subordinate's own style tended to be discursive and exploratory. He would often digress from the topic at hand to deal with background factors, alternative approaches, and so forth. His boss, instead, preferred to discuss problems with a minimum of background detail and became impatient and distracted whenever his subordinate digressed from the immediate issue.

Recognizing this difference in style, the manager became terser and more direct during meetings with his boss. To help himself do this, before meetings with the boss he would develop brief agendas that he used as a guide. Whenever he felt that a digression was needed, he explained why. This small shift in his own style made these meetings more effective and far less frustrating for them both.

Subordinates can adjust their styles in response to their bosses' preferred method for receiving information. Peter Drucker divides bosses into "listeners" and "readers." Some bosses like to get information in report form so that they can read and study it. Others work better with information and reports presented in person so that they can ask questions. As Drucker points out, the implications are obvious. If your boss is a listener, you brief him in person, *then* follow it up with a memo. If your boss is a reader, you cover important items or proposals in a memo or report, *then* discuss them with him.

Other adjustments can be made according to a boss's decision-making style. Some bosses prefer to be involved in decisions and problems as they arise. These are high-involvement managers who like to keep their hands on the pulse of the operation. Usually their needs (and your own) are best satisfied if you touch base with them on an ad hoc basis. A boss who has a need to be involved will become involved one way or another, so there are advantages to including him at your initiative. Other bosses prefer to delegate—they don't want to be involved. They expect you to come to them with major problems and inform them of important changes.

Creating a compatible relationship also involves drawing on each other's strengths and making up for each other's weaknesses. Because he knew that his boss—the vice president of engineering—was not very good at monitoring his employees' problems, one manager we studied made a point of doing it himself. The stakes were high: the engineers and technicians were all union members, the company worked on a customer-contract basis, and the company had recently experienced a serious strike.

The manager worked closely with his boss, the scheduling department, and the personnel office to ensure that potential problems were avoided. He also developed an informal arrangement through which his boss would review with him any proposed changes in personnel or assignment policies before taking action. The boss valued his advice and credited his subordinate for improving both the performance of the division and the labor-management climate.

Mutual expectations

The subordinate who passively assumes that he or she knows what the boss expects is in for trouble. Of course, some superiors will spell out their expectations very explicitly and in great detail. But most do not. And although many corporations have systems that provide a basis for communicating expectations (such as formal planning processes, career planning reviews, and performance appraisal reviews), these systems never work perfectly. Also, between these formal reviews expectations invariably change.

Ultimately, the burden falls on the subordinate to find out what the boss's expectations are. These expectations can be both broad (regarding, for example, what kinds of problems the boss wishes to be informed about and when) as well as very specific (regarding such things as when a particular project should be completed and what kinds of information the boss needs in the interim).

Getting a boss who tends to be vague or nonexplicit to express his expectations can be difficult. But effective managers find ways to get that information. Some will draft a detailed memo covering key aspects of their work and then send it to their bosses for approval. They then follow this up with a face-to-face discussion in which they go over each item in the memo. This discussion often surfaces virtually all of the boss's relevant expectations.

Exhibit
Managing the relationship with your boss

Make sure you understand your boss and his context, including:

His goals and objectives

The pressures on him

His strengths, weaknesses, blind spots

His preferred work style

Assess yourself and your needs, including:

Your own strengths and weaknesses

Your personal style

Your predisposition toward dependence on authority figures

Develop and maintain a relationship that:

Fits both your needs and styles

Is characterized by mutual expectations

Keeps your boss informed

Is based on dependability and honesty

Selectively uses your boss's time and resources

Other effective managers will deal with an inexplicit boss by initiating an ongoing series of informal discussions about "good management" and "our objectives." Still others find useful information more indirectly through those who used to work for the boss and through the formal planning systems in which the boss makes commitments to his superior. Which approach you choose, of course, should depend on your understanding of your boss's style.

Developing a workable set of mutual expectations also requires that you communicate your own expectations to the boss, find out if they are realistic, and influence the boss to accept the ones that are important to you. Being able to influence the boss to value your expectations can be particularly important if the boss is an overachiever. Such a boss will often set unrealistically high standards that need to be brought into line with reality.

A flow of information

How much information a boss needs about what a subordinate is doing will vary significantly depending on the boss's style, the situation he is in, and the confidence he has in the subordinate. But it is not uncommon for a boss to need more information than the subordinate would naturally supply or for the subordinate to think the boss knows more than he really does. Effective managers recognize that they probably underestimate what the boss needs to know and make sure they find ways to keep him informed through a process that fits his style.

Managing the flow of information upward is particularly difficult if the boss does not like to hear about problems. Although many would deny it, bosses often give off signals that they want to hear only good news. They show great displeasure—usually nonverbally—when someone tells them about a problem. Ignoring individual achievement, they may even evaluate more favorably subordinates who do not bring problems to them.

Nevertheless—for the good of the organization, boss, and subordinate—a superior needs to hear about failures as well as successes. Some subordinates deal with a good-news-only boss by finding indirect ways to get the necessary information to him, such as a management information system in which there is no messenger to be killed. Others see to it that potential problems, whether in the form of good surprises or bad news, are communicated immediately.

Dependability & honesty

Few things are more disabling to a boss than a subordinate on whom he cannot depend, whose work he cannot trust. Almost no one is intentionally undependable, but many managers are inadvertently so because of oversight or uncertainty about the boss's priorities. A commitment to an optimistic delivery date may please a superior in the short term but be a source of displeasure if not honored. It's difficult for a boss to rely on a subordinate who repeatedly slips deadlines. As one president put it (describing a subordinate): "When he's great, he's terrific, but I can't depend on him. I'd rather he be more consistent even if he delivered fewer peak successes—at least I could rely on him."

Nor are many managers intentionally dishonest with their bosses. But it is so easy to shade the truth a bit and play down concerns. Current concerns often become future surprise problems. It's almost impossible for bosses to work effectively if they cannot rely on a fairly accurate reading from their subordinates. Because it undermines credibility, dishonesty is perhaps the most troubling trait a subordinate can have. Without a basic level of trust in a subordinate's word, a boss feels he has to check all of a subordinate's decisions, which makes it difficult to delegate.

Good use of time & resources

Your boss is probably as limited in his store of time, energy, and influence as you are. Every request you make of him uses up some of these resources. For this reason, common sense suggests drawing on these resources with some selectivity. This may sound obvious, but it is surprising how many managers use up their boss's time (and some of their own credibility) over relatively trivial issues.

In one instance, a vice president went to great lengths to get his boss to fire a meddlesome secretary in another department. His boss had to use considerable effort and influence to do it. Understandably, the head of the other department was not pleased. Later, when the vice president wanted to tackle other more important problems that required changes in the scheduling and control practices of the other department, he ran into trouble. He had used up many of his own as well as his boss's blue chips on the relatively trivial issue of getting the secretary fired, thereby making it difficult for him and his boss to meet more important goals.

Whose job is it?

No doubt, some subordinates will resent that on top of all their other duties, they also need to take time and energy to manage their relationships with their bosses. Such managers fail to realize the importance of this activity and how it can simplify their jobs by eliminating potentially severe problems. Effective managers recognize that this part of their work is legitimate. Seeing themselves as ultimately responsible for what they achieve in an organization, they know they need to establish and manage relationships with everyone on whom they are dependent, and that includes the boss.▽

Reprint 80104

Pygmalion in Management

by J. Sterling Livingston

A manager's expectations are the key to a subordinate's performance and development.

In George Bernard Shaw's *Pygmalion*, Eliza Doolittle explains:

"You see, really and truly, apart from the things anyone can pick up (the dressing and the proper way of speaking, and so on), the difference between a lady and a flower girl is not how she behaves but how she's treated. I shall always be a flower girl to Professor Higgins because he always treats me as a flower girl and always will; but I know I can be a lady to you because you always treat me as a lady and always will."

Some managers always treat their subordinates in a way that leads to superior performance. But most

---

Pygmalion was a sculptor in Greek mythology who carved a statue of a beautiful woman that subsequently was brought to life. The notion that one person can transform another is the basis for this "classic" article. At the time he wrote it for the July-August 1969 issue, J. Sterling Livingston was a professor of business administration at the Harvard Business School. He had founded the Sterling Institute, a management consulting firm, in 1967. He is now chairman of the Washington, D.C.-based institute, which specializes in executive training and development.

managers, like Professor Higgins, unintentionally treat their subordinates in a way that leads to lower performance than they are capable of achieving. The way managers treat their subordinates is subtly influenced by what they expect of them. If managers'

Enthusiasm and apathy—both are infectious.

---

expectations are high, productivity is likely to be excellent. If their expectations are low, productivity is likely to be poor. It is as though there were a law that caused subordinates' performance to rise or fall to meet managers' expectations.

The powerful influence of one person's expectations on another's behavior has long been recognized by physicians and behavioral scientists and, more recently, by teachers. But heretofore the importance of managerial expectations for individual and group performance has not been widely understood. I have documented this phenomenon in a number of case studies prepared during the past decade for major industrial concerns. These cases and other evidence available from scientific research now reveal:

■ What managers expect of their subordinates and the way they treat them largely determine their performance and career progress.

■ A unique characteristic of superior managers is the ability to create high performance expectations that subordinates fulfill.

■ Less effective managers fail to develop similar expectations, and as a consequence, the productivity of their subordinates suffers.

■ Subordinates, more often than not, appear to do what they believe they are expected to do.

Impact on Productivity

One of the most comprehensive illustrations of the effect of managerial expectations on productivity is recorded in studies of the organizational experiment undertaken in 1961 by Alfred Oberlander, manager of the Rockaway district office of the Metropolitan Life Insurance Company. He had observed that outstanding insurance agencies grew faster than average or poor agencies and that new insurance agents performed better in outstanding agencies than in average or poor agencies, regardless of their sales aptitude. He decided, therefore, to group his superior agents in one unit to stimulate their performance and to provide a challenging environment in which to introduce new salespeople.

Accordingly, Oberlander assigned his six best agents to work with his best assistant manager, an equal number of average producers to work with an average assistant manager, and the remaining low producers to work with the least able manager. He then asked the superior group to produce two-thirds of the premium volume achieved by the entire agency during the previous year. He describes the results as follows:

"Shortly after this selection had been made, the people in the agency began referring to this select group as a 'superstaff' because of their high esprit de corps in operating so well as a unit. Their production efforts over the first 12 weeks far surpassed our most optimistic expectations...proving that groups of people of sound ability can be motivated beyond their apparently normal productive capacities when the problems created by the poor producer are eliminated from the operation.

"Thanks to this fine result, our overall agency performance improved by 40% and it remained at this figure.

"In the beginning of 1962 when, through expansion, we appointed another assistant manager and assigned him a staff, we again used this same concept, arranging the agents once more according to their productive capacity.

"The assistant managers were assigned...according to their ability, with the most capable assistant manager receiving the best group, thus playing strength to strength. Our agency overall production again improved by about 25% to 30%, and so this staff arrangement remained in place until the end of the year.

"Now in this year of 1963, we found upon analysis that there were so many agents...with a potential of half a million dollars or more that only one staff remained of those people in the agency who were not considered to have any chance of reaching the half-million-dollar mark."

Although the productivity of the "superstaff" improved dramatically, it should be pointed out that the productivity of those in the lowest unit, "who were not considered to have any chance of reaching the half-million-dollar mark," actually declined, and that attrition among them increased. The performance of the superior agents rose to meet their managers' expectations, while that of the weaker ones declined as predicted.

Self-Fulfilling Prophecies. The "average" unit, however, proved to be an anomaly. Although the district manager expected only average performance from this group, its productivity increased significantly. This was because the assistant manager in charge of the group refused to believe that she was less capable than the manager of the superstaff or that the agents in the top group had any greater abil-

■ **Salespeople treated by their bosses as "superstaff" try to live up to that image.**

ity than the agents in her group. She insisted in discussions with her agents that every person in the middle group had greater potential than those in the superstaff, lacking only their years of experience in selling insurance. She stimulated her agents to accept the challenge of outperforming the superstaff. As a result, in each year the middle group increased its productivity by a higher percentage than the superstaff did (although it never attained the dollar volume of the top group).

It is of special interest that the self-image of the manager of the "average" unit did not permit her to accept others' treatment of her as an "average" manager, just as Eliza Doolittle's image of herself as a lady did not permit her to accept others' treatment of her as a flower girl. The assistant manager transmitted her own strong feelings of efficacy to her agents, created mutual expectancy of high performance, and greatly stimulated productivity.

Comparable results occurred when a similar experiment was made at another office of the company. Further confirmation comes from a study of the early managerial success of 49 college graduates who were management-level employees of an operating company of AT&T. David E. Berlew and Douglas T. Hall of the Massachusetts Institute of Technology examined the career progress of these managers over a period of five years and discovered that their relative success, as measured by salary increases and the company's estimate of each one's performance and potential, depended largely on the company's expectations of them.

The influence of one person's expectations on another's behavior is by no means a business discovery. More than half a century ago, Albert Moll concluded from his clinical experience that subjects behaved as they believed they were expected to. The phenomenon he observed, in which "the prophecy causes its own fulfillment," has recently become a subject of considerable scientific interest. For example:

■ In a series of scientific experiments, Robert Rosenthal of Harvard University has demonstrated that a "teacher's expectation for a pupil's intellectual competence can come to serve as an educational self-fulfilling prophecy."

■ An experiment in a summer Headstart program for 60 preschoolers compared the performance of pupils under (a) teachers who had been led to expect relatively slow learning by their children, and (b) teachers who had been led to believe that their children had excellent intellectual ability and learning capacity. Pupils of the second group of teachers learned much faster.[1]

Moreover, the healing professions have long recognized that a physician's or psychiatrist's expectations can have a formidable influence on a patient's physical or mental health. What takes place in the minds of the patients and the healers, particularly when they have congruent expectations, may determine the outcome. For instance, the havoc of a doctor's pessimistic prognosis has often been observed. Again, it is well known that the efficacy of a new drug or a new treatment can be greatly influenced by the physician's expectations—a result referred to by the medical profession as a "placebo effect."

Pattern of Failure. When salespersons are treated by their managers as superpeople, as the superstaff was at the Metropolitan Rockaway district office,

they try to live up to that image and do what they know supersalespersons are expected to do. But when the agents with poor productivity records are treated by their managers as *not* having "any chance" of success, as the low producers at Rockaway were, this negative expectation also becomes a managerial self-fulfilling prophecy.

Unsuccessful salespersons have great difficulty maintaining their self-image and self-esteem. In response to low managerial expectations, they typically attempt to prevent additional damage to their egos by avoiding situations that might lead to greater failure. They either reduce the number of sales calls they make or avoid trying to "close" sales when that might result in further painful rejection, or both. Low expectations and damaged egos lead them to behave in a manner that increases the probability of failure, thereby fulfilling their managers' expectations. Let me illustrate:

Not long ago I studied the effectiveness of branch bank managers at a West Coast bank with over 500 branches. The managers who had had their lending authority reduced because of high rates of loss became progressively less effective. To prevent further loss of authority, they turned to making only "safe"

COUNTERPRODUCTION DEPARTMENT

D. Fradon

loans. This action resulted in losses of business to competing banks and a relative decline in both deposits and profits at their branches. Then, to reverse that decline in deposits and earnings, they often "reached" for loans and became almost irrational in their acceptance of questionable credit risks. Their actions were not so much a matter of poor judgment as an expression of their willingness to take desperate risks in the hope of being able to avoid further damage to their egos and to their careers.

Thus, in response to the low expectations of their supervisors who had reduced their lending authority, they behaved in a manner that led to larger credit losses. They appeared to do what they believed they were expected to do, and their supervisors' expectations became self-fulfilling prophecies.

Power of Expectations

Managers cannot avoid the depressing cycle of events that flow from low expectations merely by hiding their feelings from subordinates. If managers believe subordinates will perform poorly, it is virtually impossible for them to mask their expectations because the message usually is communicated unintentionally, without conscious action on their part.

Indeed, managers often communicate most when they believe they are communicating least. For instance, when they say nothing—become cold and uncommunicative—it usually is a sign that they are displeased by a subordinate or believe that he or she is hopeless. The silent treatment communicates negative feelings even more effectively, at times, than a tongue-lashing does. What seems to be critical in the communication of expectations is not what the boss says so much as the way he or she behaves. Indifferent and noncommital treatment, more often than not, is the kind of treatment that communicates low expectations and leads to poor performance.

Common Illusions. Managers are more effective in communicating low expectations to their subordinates than in communicating high expectations to them, even though most managers believe exactly the opposite. It usually is astonishingly difficult for them to recognize the clarity with which they transmit negative feelings. To illustrate again:

■ The Rockaway district manager vigorously denied that he had communicated low expectations to the agents in the poorest group who, he believed, did not have "any chance" of becoming high producers. Yet the message was clearly received by those agents. A typical case was that of an agent who resigned from the low unit. When the district manager told the

agent that he was sorry she was leaving, the agent replied, "No you're not; you're glad." Although the district manager previously had said nothing to her, he had unintentionally communicated his low expectations to his agents through his indifferent manner. Subsequently, the agents who were assigned to the lowest unit interpreted the assignment as equivalent to a request for their resignation.

■ One of the company's agency managers established superior, average, and low units, even though he was convinced that he had no superior or outstanding subordinates. "All my assistant managers and agents are either average or incompetent," he explained to the Rockaway district manager. Although he tried to duplicate the Rockaway results, his low opinions of his agents were communicated—not so subtly—to them. As a result, the experiment failed.

Positive feelings, on the other hand, often do not come through clearly enough. Another insurance agency manager copied the organizational changes made at the Rockaway district office, grouping the salespeople she rated highly with the best manager, the average salespeople with an average manager, and so on. Improvement, however, did not result from the move. The Rockaway district manager therefore investigated the situation. He discovered that the assistant manager in charge of the high-performance unit was unaware that his manager considered him to be the best. In fact, he and the other agents doubted that the agency manager really believed there was any difference in their abilities. This agency manager was a stolid, phlegmatic, unemotional woman who treated her agents in a rather pedestrian way. Since high expectations had not been communicated to them, they did not understand the reason for the new organization and could not see any point in it. Clearly, the way managers *treat* subordinates, not the way they organize them, is the key to high expectations and high productivity.

Impossible Dreams. Managerial expectations must pass the test of reality before they can be translated into performance. To become self-fulfilling prophecies, expectations must be made of sterner stuff than the power of positive thinking or generalized confidence in one's subordinates— helpful as these concepts may be for some other purposes. Subordinates will not be motivated to reach high levels of productivity unless they consider the boss's high expectations realistic and achievable. If they are encouraged to strive for unattainable goals, they eventually give up trying and settle for results that are lower than they are capable of achieving. The experience of a large electrical manufacturing company demonstrates this; the company discovered that production actually declined if production quo-

Retrospective Commentary

J. Sterling Livingston

Self-fulfilling managerial prophecies were a bit mysterious when I documented the phenomenon 19 years ago. At that time, the powerful influence of managers' expectations on the development, motivation, and performance of their subordinates was not widely understood. Since then, however, the "Pygmalion effect" has become well known.

Recent research has confirmed that effective leaders have the ability to create high performance expectations that their employees fulfill. Every manager should understand, therefore, how the Pygmalion effect works.

What managers think about themselves and their abilities, as I explained in "Pygmalion In Management," is crucial to their effectiveness in creating self-fulfilling prophecies. Warren Bennis and Burt Nanus recently reached a similar conclusion after conducting some 90 interviews with CEOs and top public administrators. They wrote: "Our study of effective leaders strongly suggested that a key factor was …what we're calling…positive self-regard….Positive self-regard seems to exert its force by creating in others a sense of confidence and high expectations, not very different from the fabled Pygmalion effect."*

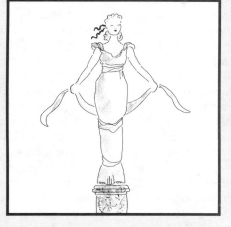

The way managers develop confidence in their abilities and transmit their feelings of efficacy to their employees is illustrated by the success of Lee A. Iacocca of Chrysler—whom, interestingly, Bennis and Nanus used as a model for their theory of leadership. Iacocca's self-assurance can be traced to his prior success as president of Ford. His subsequent prophecy that Chrysler would be saved was accepted as credible by Chrysler's employees because they saw him as a competent automobile executive. They tried hard to meet his expectations and "behaved as they believed they were expected to," which my article indicated would be normal under the circumstances.

It is highly unlikely, however, that Iacocca could have saved Chrysler if he had been an industry outsider who needed two or three years to learn the automotive business. If he had been an outsider, he could not have moved decisively to do what needed to be done, nor could he have created a strong sense of confidence and high expectations among Chrysler's employees. His success was due to his experience and competence. It is doubtful that a prophecy by a less-qualified executive would have been self-fulfilling. So the message for managers is this: to be a Pygmalion, you must acquire the industry knowledge and job skills required to be confident of your high expectations and to make them credible to your employees.

Your organization can help identify the knowledge and skills you need to perform your job effectively. Your supervisors can give you assignments that will spur your development. But you must assume responsibility for your own development and career growth.

A word of caution may be in order, however. As I explained in my article, managers often unintentionally communicate low expectations to their subordinates, even though they believe otherwise. When they communicate low expectations, they become "negative" Pygmalions who undermine the self-confidence of their employees and reduce their effectiveness. Managers must be extremely sensitive, therefore, to their own behavior and its impact on their subordinates. They must guard against treating their employees in ways that lower their feelings of efficacy and self-esteem and are unproductive.

If I were writing "Pygmalion in Management" today, I might focus more attention on the problems of the negative Pygmalions because there are more of them than positive Pygmalions in U.S. industry. But the dark side of the Pygmalion effect is distressing, and I prefer to think about the bright side. It is a hopeful concept that can help all managers become more effective.

The difference between employees who perform well and those who perform poorly is not how they are paid but how they are treated. All managers can learn how to treat their employees in ways that will lead to mutual expectations of superior performance. The most effective managers always do.

---

*Reported in their book *Leaders* (New York: Harper & Row, 1985).

tas were set too high, because the workers simply stopped trying to meet them. In other words, the practice of "dangling the carrot just beyond the donkey's reach," endorsed by many managers, is not a good motivational device.

Scientific research by David C. McClelland of Harvard University and John W. Atkinson of the University of Michigan has demonstrated that the relationship of motivation to expectancy varies in the form of a bell-shaped curve (see the exhibit).[2]

Indifference says to subordinates, "I don't think much of you."

The degree of motivation and effort rises until the expectancy of success reaches 50%, then begins to fall even though the expectancy of success continues to increase. No motivation or response is aroused when the goal is perceived as being either virtually certain or virtually impossible to attain.

Moreover, as Berlew and Hall have pointed out, if subordinates fail to meet performance expectations that are close to their own level of aspirations, they will lower personal performance goals and standards, performance will tend to drop off, and negative attitudes will develop toward the activity or job.[3] It is therefore not surprising that failure of subordinates to meet the unrealistically high expectations of their managers leads to high rates of attrition, either voluntary or involuntary.

Secret of Superiority. Something takes place in the minds of superior managers that does not occur in the minds of those who are less effective. While superior managers are consistently able to create high performance expectations that their subordinates fulfill, weaker managers are not successful in obtaining a similar response. What accounts for the difference?

The answer, in part, seems to be that superior managers have greater confidence than other managers in their own ability to develop the talents of their subordinates. Contrary to what might be assumed, the high expectations of superior managers are based primarily on what they think about themselves—about their own ability to select, train, and motivate their subordinates. What managers believe about themselves subtly influences what they believe about their subordinates, what they expect of them, and how they treat them. If they have confidence in their ability to develop and stimulate them to high levels of performance, they will expect much of them and will treat them with confidence that their expecta-

tions will be met. But if they have doubts about their ability to stimulate them, they will expect less of them and will treat them with less confidence.

Stated in another way, the superior managers' record of success and their confidence in their ability give their high expectations credibility. As a consequence, their subordinates accept these expectations as realistic and try hard to achieve them.

The importance of what a manager believes about his or her training and motivational ability is illustrated by "Sweeney's Miracle," a managerial and educational self-fulfilling prophecy.

James Sweeney taught industrial management and psychiatry at Tulane University, and he also was responsible for the operation of the Biomedical Computer Center there. Sweeney believed that he could teach even a poorly educated man to be a capable computer operator. George Johnson, a former hospital porter, became janitor at the computer center; he was chosen by Sweeney to prove his conviction. In the mornings, George Johnson performed his janitorial duties, and in the afternoons Sweeney taught him about computers.

Johnson was learning a great deal about computers when someone at the university concluded that to be a computer operator one had to have a certain I.Q. score. Johnson was tested, and his I.Q. indicated that he would not be able to learn to type, much less operate a computer.

But Sweeney was not convinced. He threatened to quit unless Johnson was permitted to learn to program and operate the computer. Sweeney prevailed, and he is still running the computer center. Johnson is now in charge of the main computer room and is responsible for training new employees to program and operate the computer.[4]

Sweeney's expectations were based on what he believed about his own teaching ability, not on Johnson's learning credentials. What managers believe about their ability to train and motivate subordinates clearly is the foundation on which realistically high managerial expectations are built.

The Critical Early Years

Managerial expectations have their most magical influence on young people. As subordinates mature and gain experience, their self-image gradually hardens, and they begin to see themselves as their career records imply. Their own aspirations and the expectations of their superiors become increasingly controlled by the "reality" of their past performance. It becomes more and more difficult for them and for

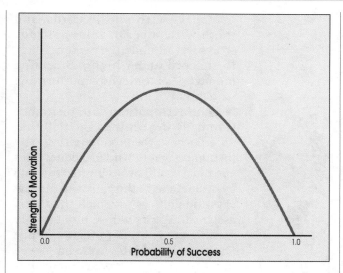

their managers to generate mutually high expectations unless they have outstanding records.

Incidentally, the same pattern occurs in school. Rosenthal's experiments with educational self-fulfilling prophecies consistently demonstrate that teachers' expectations are more effective in influencing intellectual growth in younger children than in older children. In the lower grade levels, particularly in the first and second grades, the effects of teachers' expectations are dramatic. In the upper grade levels, teachers' prophecies seem to have little effect on children's intellectual growth, although they do affect their motivation and attitude toward school. While the declining influence of teachers' expectations cannot be completely explained, it is reasonable to conclude that younger children are more malleable, have fewer fixed notions about their abilities, and have less well-established reputations in the schools. As they grow, particularly if they are assigned to "tracks" on the basis of their records, as is now often done in public schools, their beliefs about their intellectual ability and their teachers' expectations of them begin to harden and become more resistant to influence by others.

Key to Future Performance. The early years in a business organization, when young people can be strongly influenced by managerial expectations, are critical in determining future performance and career progress. This is shown by a study at AT&T.

Berlew and Hall found that what the company initially expected of 49 college graduates who were management-level employees was the most critical factor in their subsequent performance and success. The researchers concluded that the correlation between how much a company expects of an employee in the first year and how much that employee contributes during the next five years was "too compelling to be ignored."[5]

Subsequently, the two men studied the career records of 18 college graduates who were hired as management trainees in another of AT&T's operating companies. Again they found that both expectations and performance in the first year correlated consistently with later performance and success.

"Something important is happening in the first year...," Berlew and Hall concluded. "Meeting high company expectations in the critical first year leads to the internalization of positive job attitudes and high standards; these attitudes and standards, in turn, would first lead to and be reinforced by strong performance and success in later years. It should also follow that a new manager who meets the challenge of one highly demanding job will be given subsequently a more demanding job, and his level of contribution will rise as he responds to the company's growing expectations of him. The key...is the concept of the first year as a *critical period for learning,* a time when the trainee is uniquely ready to develop or change in the direction of the company's expectations."[6]

Most Influential Boss. A young person's first manager is likely to be the most influential in that person's career. If managers are unable or unwilling to develop the skills young employees need to perform effectively, the latter will set lower personal standards than they are capable of achieving, their self-images will be impaired, and they will develop negative attitudes toward jobs, employers, and—in all probability—their own careers in business. Since the chances of building successful careers with these first employers will decline rapidly, the employees will leave, if they have high aspirations, in hope of finding better opportunities. If, on the other hand, early managers help employees achieve maximum potential, they will build the foundations for successful careers.

With few exceptions, the most effective branch managers at a large West Coast bank were mature people in their forties and fifties. The bank's executives explained that it took considerable time for a person to gain the knowledge, experience, and judgment required to handle properly credit risks, customer relations, and employee relations.

One branch manager, however, ranked in the top 10% of the managers in terms of effectiveness (which included branch profit growth, deposit growth, scores on administrative audits, and subjective rankings by superiors), was only 27 years old. This young person had been made a branch manager at 25, and in two years had improved not only the performance of the branch substantially but also developed a younger assistant manager who, in turn, was made a branch manager at 25.

"Instead of my usual report, I've written a little song about our accounting procedure, our lack of cash flow, and why the business is going to hell in a handbasket. Feel free to jump in on the chorus."

managers with poor records, and those with superior sales aptitude scores were found to be twice as likely to succeed under high-performing managers as under low-performing managers.[7]

■ The Metropolitan Life Insurance Company determined in 1960 that differences in the productivity of new insurance agents who had equal sales aptitudes could be accounted for only by differences in the ability of managers in the offices to which they were assigned. Agents whose productivity was high in relation to their aptitude test scores invariably were employed in offices that had production records among the top third in the company. Conversely, those whose productivity was low in relation to their test scores typically were in the least successful offices. After analyzing all the factors that might have accounted for these variations, the company concluded that differences in the performance of new agents were due primarily to differences in the "proficiency in sales training and direction" of the local managers.[8]

The assistant had had only average grades in college, but in just four years at the bank had been assigned to work with two branch managers who were remarkably effective teachers. The first boss, who was recognized throughout the bank for unusual skill in developing young people, did not believe that it took years to gain the knowledge and skill needed to become an effective banker. After two years, the young person was made assistant manager at a branch headed by another executive, who also was an effective developer of subordinates. Thus it was that the young person, when promoted to head a branch, confidently followed the model of two previous superiors in operating the branch, quickly established a record of outstanding performance, and trained an assistant to assume responsibility early.

For confirming evidence of the crucial role played by a person's first bosses, let us turn to selling, since performance in this area is more easily measured than in most managerial areas. Consider the following investigations:

■ In a study of the careers of 100 insurance salespeople who began work with either highly competent or less-than-competent agency managers, the Life Insurance Agency Management Association found that those with average sales-aptitude test scores were nearly five times as likely to succeed under managers with good performance records as under

■ A study I conducted of the performance of automobile salespeople in Ford dealerships in New England revealed that superior salespersons were concentrated in a few outstanding dealerships. For instance, 10 of the top 15 salespeople in New England were in 3 (out of approximately 200) of the dealerships in this region, and 5 of the top 15 people were in one highly successful dealership. Yet 4 of these people previously had worked for other dealers without achieving

> ▍ **Superior managers don't give up on themselves and don't give up easily on subordinates either.**

outstanding sales records. There was little doubt that the training and motivational skills of managers in the outstanding dealerships were critical.

Astute Selection. While success in business sometimes appears to depend on the luck of the draw, more than luck is involved when a young person is selected by a superior manager. Successful managers do not pick their subordinates at random or by the toss of a coin. They are careful to select only those who they "know" will succeed. As Metropolitan's

Rockaway district manager, Alfred Oberlander, insisted: "Every man or woman who starts with us is going to be a top-notch life insurance agent, or he or she would not have been asked to join the team."

When pressed to explain how they "know" whether a person will be successful, superior managers usually end up by saying something like, "The qualities are intangible, but I know them when I see them." They have difficulty being explicit because their selection process is intuitive and is based on interpersonal intelligence that is difficult to describe. The key seems to be that they are able to identify subordinates with whom they can probably work effectively—people with whom they are compatible and whose body chemistry agrees with their own. They make mistakes, of course. But they "give up" on a subordinate slowly because that means "giving up" on themselves—on their judgment and ability in selecting, training, and motivating people. Less effective managers select subordinates more quickly and give up on them more easily, believing that the inadequacy is that of the subordinate, not of themselves.

Developing Young People

Observing that his company's research indicates that "initial corporate expectations for performance (with real responsibility) mold subsequent expectations and behavior," R.W. Walters, Jr., director of college employment at AT&T, contends that "initial bosses of new college hires must be the best in the organization."[9] Unfortunately, however, most companies practice exactly the opposite.

Rarely do new graduates work closely with experienced middle managers or upper-level executives. Normally they are bossed by first-line managers who tend to be the least experienced and least effective in the organization. While there are exceptions, first-line managers generally are either "old pros" who have been judged as lacking competence for higher levels of responsibility, or they are younger people who are making the transition from "doing" to "managing." Often these managers lack the knowledge and skill required to develop the productive capabilities of their subordinates. As a consequence, many college graduates begin their careers in business under the worst possible circumstances. Since they know their abilities are not being developed or used, they quite naturally soon become negative toward their jobs, employers, and business careers.

Although most top executives have not yet diagnosed the problem, industry's greatest challenge by far is to rectify the underdevelopment, underutilization, and ineffective management and use of its most valuable resource—its young managerial and professional talent.

Disillusion and Turnover. The problem posed to corporate management is underscored by the sharply rising rates of attrition among young managerial and professional personnel. Turnover among managers one to five years out of college is almost twice as high

We all are like Eliza Doolittle — we behave according to how we're treated.

now as it was a decade ago, and five times as high as two decades ago. Three out of five companies surveyed by *Fortune* magazine in the fall of 1968 reported that turnover rates among young managers and professionals were higher than five years ago.[10] While the high level of economic activity and the shortage of skilled personnel have made job-hopping easier, the underlying causes of high attrition, I am convinced, are underdevelopment and underutilization of a work force that has high career aspirations.

The problem can be seen in its extreme form in the excessive attrition rates of college and university graduates who begin their careers in sales positions. Whereas the average company loses about 50% of its new college and university graduates within three to five years, attrition rates as high as 40% in the *first* year are common among college graduates who accept sales positions in the average company. This attrition stems primarily, in my opinion, from the failure of first-line managers to teach new college recruits what they need to know to be effective sales representatives.

As we have seen, young people who begin their careers working for less-than-competent sales managers are likely to have records of low productivity. When rebuffed by their customers and considered by their managers to have little potential for success, the young people naturally have great difficulty in maintaining their self-esteem. Soon they find little personal satisfaction in their jobs and, to avoid further loss of self-respect, leave their employers for jobs that look more promising. Moreover, as reports about the high turnover and disillusionment of those who embarked on sales careers filter back to college campuses, new graduates become increasingly reluctant to take jobs in sales.

Thus ineffective first-line sales management sets off a sequence of events that ends with college and university graduates avoiding careers in selling. To a lesser extent, the same pattern is duplicated in other functions of business, as evidenced by the growing trend of college graduates to pursue careers in "more meaningful" occupations, such as teaching and government service.

A serious "generation gap" between bosses and subordinates is another significant cause of breakdown. Many managers resent the abstract, academic language and narrow rationalization characteristically used by recent graduates. As one manager expressed it to me, "For God's sake, you need a lexicon even to talk with these kids." Nondegreed managers often are particularly resentful, perhaps because they feel threatened by the bright young people with book-learned knowledge that they do not understand.

For whatever reason, the "generation gap" in many companies is eroding managerial expectations of new college graduates. For instance, I know of a survey of management attitudes in one of the nation's largest companies that revealed that 54% of its first-line and second-line managers believed that new college recruits were "not as good as they were five years ago." Since what managers expect of subordinates influences the way they treat them, it is understandable that new graduates often develop negative attitudes toward their jobs and their employers. Clearly, low managerial expectations and hostile attitudes are not the basis for effective management of new people entering business.

Industry has not developed effective first-line managers fast enough to meet its needs. As a consequence, many companies are underdeveloping their most valuable resource—talented young men and women. They are incurring heavy attrition costs and contributing to the negative attitudes young people often have about careers in business.

For top executives in industry who are concerned with the productivity of their organizations and the careers of young employees, the challenge is clear: to speed the development of managers who will treat subordinates in ways that lead to high performance and career satisfaction. Managers not only shape the expectations and productivity of their subordinates but also influence their attitudes toward their jobs and themselves. If managers are unskilled, they leave scars on the careers of young people, cut deeply into their self-esteem, and distort their image of themselves as human beings. But if they are skillful and have high expectations, subordinates' self-confidence will grow, their capabilities will develop, and their productivity will be high. More often than one realizes, the manager is Pygmalion.

References

1. The Rosenthal and Headstart studies are cited in Robert Rosenthal and Lenore Jacobson, *Pygmalion in the Classroom* (New York: Holt, Rinehart, and Winston, Inc., 1968) p.11.

2. See John W. Atkinson, "Motivational Determinants of Risk-Taking Behavior," *Psychological Review*, vol. 64, no. 6, 1957, p. 365.

3. David E. Berlew and Douglas T. Hall, "The Socialization of Managers: Effects of Expectations on Performance," *Administrative Science Quarterly*, September 1966, p. 208.

4. See Rosenthal and Jacobson, *Pygmalion in the Classroom*, p. 3.

5. Berlew and Hall, "The Socialization of Managers," p. 221.

6. David E. Berlew and Douglas T. Hall, "Some Determinants of Early Managerial Success," Alfred P. Sloan School of Management Organization Research Program #81-64 (Cambridge: MIT, 1964), p. 13.

7. Robert T. Davis, "Sales Management in the Field," HBR January-February 1958, p. 91.

8. Alfred A. Oberlander, "The Collective Conscience in Recruiting," address to Life Insurance Agency Management Association annual meeting, Chicago, Illinois, 1963, p. 5.

9. "How to Keep the Go-Getters," *Nation's Business*, June 1966, p. 74.

10. Robert C. Albrook, "Why It's Harder to Keep Good Executives," *Fortune*, November 1968, p. 137.

Reprint 88509

*How to overcome
the limits of trust and the
fear of candor*

Nobody Trusts the Boss Completely— Now What?

by Fernando Bartolomé

Managers who can head off serious problems before they blow up in the company's face are two steps ahead of the game. Their employers avoid needless expense or outright disaster, and they themselves get the promotions they deserve for running their departments smoothly and nipping trouble neatly in the bud.

 Subordinates are never eager to give the boss bad news.

In practice, of course, it's never this easy. Everyone knows that one trick to dealing with problems is to learn about them early. But what's the trick to learning about them early? How do effective managers find out that trouble is brewing? What are their warning systems?

All good managers have their own private information networks, and many develop a kind of sixth sense for the early signs of trouble. But by far the simplest and most common way to find out about problems is to be told, usually by a subordinate.

It is easy to get information when things are going well. People love to give the boss good news. But subordinates are never eager to tell their supervisors that the latest scheme isn't working, to assume ownership of a problem by giving it a name, to look like an informer, or to sound like Chicken Little. A subordinate's reluctance to be frank about problems is also related to risk. While it's fairly easy to tell the boss that the machines sent over by the purchasing department aren't working properly, it's much harder to admit responsibility for the malfunction, and harder still—and perhaps dangerous—to blame it on the boss. Yet it is terribly important to get subordinates to convey unpleasant messages. The sooner a problem is disclosed, diagnosed, and corrected, the better for the company.

Almost any organization would operate more effectively with completely open and forthright employees, but absolute frankness is too much to hope for (and probably too much to bear). Candor depends upon trust, and in hierarchical organizations, trust has strict natural limits.

The Limits of Trust and Candor

In a hierarchy, it is natural for people with less power to be extremely cautious about disclosing weaknesses, mistakes, and failings—especially when the more powerful party is also in a position to evaluate and punish. Trust flees authority, and, above all, trust flees a judge. Managers are inescapably positioned to judge subordinates. Good managers may be able to confine evaluation to formal occasions, to avoid all trace of judgmental style in other settings, even to communicate criticism in a positive, constructive way. But there is no way to escape completely a subordinate's inclination to see superiors as judges.

So one of the limits on candor is self-protection. For example, people often hide the failures of their own departments and hope they will correct themselves. In one typical case, the development group for a piece of special software fell terribly behind on its

Fernando Bartolomé is professor of management at Bentley College in Waltham, Massachusetts. He is also guest lecturer at the European Institute of Business Administration (INSEAD) in France and at the Oxford Centre for Management Studies in England. He consults frequently in Europe, the United States, and Latin America. This is his fifth article for HBR.

"Don't you have any feeling for this car, Mr. Geller?
Don't you ever communicate with it?"

Sometimes a subordinate may try to protect a client. In one case, a salesman withheld the information that one of his largest customers was in financial trouble. The customer went bankrupt, and the company lost $500,000.

We can only guess at the salesman's motives—eagerness to get his commission before the troubled company failed, fear of losing an old customer, reluctance to give official warning of a danger that might be exaggerated. The fact remains that he failed to communicate the problem, his boss saw no sign of danger, and the company lost half a million dollars.

Often the motive for silence is at least superficially praiseworthy: people keep quiet about a developing problem while trying to solve it. Most believe solving problems on their own is what they're paid to do, and in many cases, they're right. Subordinates are not paid to run to their bosses with every glitch and hiccup. As problems grow more serious, however, managers need to know about them.

schedule, but no one told the manager until the delivery date could no longer be met. Delivery was three months late, and the company had to absorb a financial penalty.

The lack of candor was not self-protective in the long run, of course, because the development group was ultimately held responsible for the delay. But human beings are often shortsighted. At one time or another, most of us have chosen an uncertain future calamity over today's immediate unpleasantness.

A variation on this theme is when subordinates protect their own subordinates in order to protect themselves, as in the following example:

☐ I was vice president of finance for a large manufacturing company and supervised a staff of 27. One new hire was failing on an important assignment. Her supervisor—who had hired her—withheld this information from me until her failure could no longer be corrected without serious disruption. He didn't tell me because he knew I would make him face up to the problem and deal with it, which he knew he would find very difficult to do.

The difficulty here lies in the bewildering territory between minor snags and major disasters. Handled promptly and decisively, the problems in this gray area sometimes turn out to be insignificant, but self-confident supervisors, particularly inexperienced ones, are perhaps too eager to prove they can cope on their own. This case is typical:

☐ I am head of medical research in a pharmaceutical company. My job is part of R&D and is on the critical path to marketing any new product. One of my managers saw that we weren't receiving data critical to the timely generation of a licensing package for worldwide registration of a new drug. He spent four months trying to get the data on his own, or proceed without it, and didn't inform me of the problem. We suffered an eight-month delay in applying for a license to sell. That represents 10% of the patent life of the product, which has estimated peak worldwide sales of $120 million a year.

Politics is another common obstacle to candor. Organizations are political systems, and employees are often involved in political struggles. There is no guarantee your subordinates will be on your side.

A U.S. engineering-products company manufactured a successful product on license from a Swedish company, but the American CEO heartily disliked his Swedish counterpart and came to the private conclusion that the licensing fees were out of line. Knowing that his senior staff would object, he began confidential acquisition talks with one of the Swedish corporation's competitors, a much smaller and technically less sophisticated company. Because the negotiations were too complex for him to handle alone, he circumvented the vice presidents who would have opposed the move and secretly enlisted the help of their subordinates. By the time the negotiations became public, it was too late for the senior staff to stop the deal. The Swedish company canceled its license, and the U.S. company has not sold a single piece of new technology since the acquisition.

This CEO made a grave error in letting his personal feelings interfere with his business judgment, but his incompetence, however great, is not the point. The point is that certain employees concealed information from their immediate superiors. Their motives are easy to guess at and perhaps understandable—after all, they were acting on orders from the CEO. But the fact remains that not one of them spoke up, their superiors suspected nothing, and the consequences for the company were extremely negative.

In these days of mergers and acquisitions, political infighting is often acute after absorption of—or by—another company. Restructuring and consolidation can produce epidemic fear and rupture lines of communication, as this case illustrates:

☐ My electronics corporation acquired a division of another company and merged it with two existing subsidiaries. Many employees were let go in the process of the merger and consolidation. I was named president and CEO of the new company one year after its formation. The new company had its headquarters on the East Coast and its research facilities

> ## Mergers, acquisitions, and office politics can all choke off the flow of essential information.

in the West. The VP for research—whose office was in California—did not tell me that the merger, the layoffs, and the new company policies and procedures had had a terrible impact on employee morale. I was completely unaware of the problem for four months.

Then I visited the research facility to announce a new benefits package. After announcing the plan, I asked for questions. All hell broke loose. For the next year and a half I spent about a third of my time and a great deal of other people's time trying to build bridges and establish trust, hoping to lower turnover, improve productivity, and get those Californians to feel like part of the total company.

Why wasn't I told? My guess is that the subordinate who kept me in the dark was afraid for his own job. Or else he felt he had something to gain by undermining my position. I don't know, but it was an expensive failure of communication.

Building and Destroying Trust

Given the natural obstacles to trust and candor—fear, pride, politics, dislike—managers need to make the most of whatever opportunities they have to increase subordinates' trust. Trust is not easy to build in the best of cases, and the kind of trust that concerns us here has to grow on rocky ground—between people at different levels of authority.

The factors affecting the development of trust and candor fall into six categories: communication, support, respect, fairness, predictability, and competence.

Communication is a matter of keeping subordinates informed, providing accurate feedback, explaining decisions and policies, being candid about one's own problems, and resisting the temptation to hoard information for use as a tool or a reward.

For several years, the founder and CEO of a small, South American conglomerate had addressed the needs of each of his six divisions separately. He treated his vice presidents like the CEOs of the divisions, cutting deals with each of them independently and keeping each in the dark about his arrangements with the others. He had always solved problems on this ad hoc basis, and it worked reasonably well. The company had grown swiftly and steadily. But now times were tougher, the company was bigger, and he began getting complaints from his VPs about resource allocation. None of them was satisfied with his own division's share, but none was in a position to consider the needs of the company as a whole.

At this point, the CEO recognized that his way of managing was part of the problem, did an abrupt about-face, and created an executive committee comprising himself and his six VPs. They all took part in setting priorities, allocating resources, and planning company strategy. Conflicts remained, of course, as each vice president fought for resources for his division. But trust increased substantially, and for the first time there was communication between divisions and a willingness and opportunity for the company's leadership to work together as a team.

Another CEO moved the offices of his small company without notice. His staff simply arrived at work one Monday morning to learn that the movers were coming on Tuesday. When asked to explain, the man gave his reasons but clearly didn't feel his employees needed to know. He insulted and belittled the people he depended on for information and support.

It is important to communicate with subordinates not only as a group but also as individuals. This woman's boss may have believed money spoke for itself:

☐ I have been working for my current boss for two years and never had a performance appraisal. I guess I'm doing okay because I get good raises every year. But I have no idea what the future may hold for me in this company.

Middle- to upper-level managers often find it difficult to talk with superiors about their own perfor-

> ## Resist the temptation to use information as a tool or a reward.

mance and career prospects. When they feel they aren't getting the feedback they need, they are uncomfortable asking for it. Communication must flow in both directions if it is to flow at all. Information won't surge up where it barely trickles down.

Support means showing concern for subordinates as people. It means being available and approachable. It means helping people, coaching them, encouraging their ideas, and defending their positions. It may mean socializing with them. It certainly means taking an interest in their lives and careers. Here are three examples of good and poor support:

☐ During one period of my life, I had some serious personal problems that affected my work. My boss protected me at work and gave me a lot of moral support. Eventually, I was able to solve my problems, thanks in part to her help. That strengthened our professional relationship enormously.
☐ I presented a proposal to the executive committee. Some members were in favor, others against. I was so young and nervous, I didn't see how I could possibly convince them I was right. Then my boss took on the

defense of my proposal, argued energetically in favor of it, and we won. When I think back on it now, I realize that few events in my career have pleased me more or given me a more genuine sense of gratitude.
☐ I approved a credit and had been authorized by my boss to waive certain credit warranties. Then some other people started questioning what I had done and throwing doubt on my competence. Instead of supporting me, my boss took the side of my critics.

It is often tempting to abandon an employee who is in trouble, out of favor, or simply unpopular, but the extra effort expended in behalf of such a person can pay big dividends later. When you have to terminate employees, the worst possible method is to let them twist in the wind. Get rid of those you have to get rid of. Support the others for all you're worth. Subordinates trust most deeply the superiors they feel will stand by them when the chips are down.

Respect feeds on itself. The most important form of respect is delegation, and the second most important is listening to subordinates and acting on their opinions. In the first two examples below, the boss shows genuine respect for the subordinate's judgment and intelligence. In the third, the relationship actually deteriorates in the course of the meeting.

☐ My boss put me in charge of a project. It involved a big risk for me, but an even bigger risk for her if I failed. I asked her how she wanted me to do it and who else I should contact for clearance. She said, "You have free rein on this. Whatever you do is okay with me."
☐ Six years ago, just after I joined the bank, my boss told me he had decided to buy a company and asked me to look into it and give him my opinion. I did my homework and told him I thought it was a bad idea. So he eliminated me from the team he had put together to manage the acquisition. Somehow I succeeded in persuading him to listen to a fuller presentation of my analysis. He not only took the time, he really listened to my arguments and finally canceled the purchase.
☐ My boss and I agreed that we had to reduce the personnel in my department. I wanted to cut five positions; he wanted to cut eight. I argued my case for an hour. In the end he forced me to cut eight jobs, without even answering my arguments, and I realized he hadn't paid attention to anything I'd said.

In interpersonal relations, the law of reciprocity tends to rule. When supervisors use a lot of fine words about trust and respect but behave disdainfully, subordinates are likely to respond in kind.

Fairness means giving credit where it's due, being objective and impartial in performance appraisals, giving praise liberally. The opposite kind of behavior —favoritism, hypocrisy, misappropriating ideas and accomplishments, unethical behavior—is difficult to forgive and hugely destructive of trust. These two examples make the point well:

☐ One of my subordinates had what I thought was a terrific idea, and I told my boss. He agreed and immediately dictated a memo to the division manager outlining the idea and giving full credit where it was due. I learned sometime later that he never sent that memo but substituted another in which he took a good share of the credit for himself—and gave an equal share to me. I not only felt cheated, I felt I had somehow taken part in a plot to cheat the person who had the idea in the first place. It not only destroyed my relationship with that boss, it almost ruined my relationship with my subordinate.
☐ We were involved in a very difficult lawsuit with a former client. The battle lasted four years, and in the end we lost the case before the Supreme Court. When I gave the news to my boss, I was afraid he would take it badly, as a kind of personal failure. But he understood that we lost because of factors completely out of our control, and, instead of criticizing us, he praised our hard work and dedication.

Chronic lack of fairness will dry up trust and candor quickly, but every act of support and fair play will prime the pump.

Predictability is a matter of behaving consistently and dependably and of keeping both explicit and implicit promises. A broken promise can do considerable damage, as this example illustrates:

☐ When my boss hired me, she promised me a percentage of the profits on the project I was to manage. My arrival was delayed, so I took over the project as it

Not giving credit where it's due is hugely destructive of trust.

was winding down—without any profits to speak of. As soon as I cleaned up the loose ends, I took over a new project that was my responsibility from the outset. I managed it well, and profits were substantial. I felt badly cheated when I was told that my percentage deal applied to the first project only, that I had no such agreement on the second. I complained bitterly, and the company made it right. But it left a bad taste in my mouth, and I left shortly afterward.

Another form of predictability is consistency of character, which is, after all, the best proof of authenticity.

Competence, finally, means demonstrating technical and professional ability and good business sense. Employees don't want to be subordinate to people they see as incompetent. Trust grows from seeds of decent behavior, but it thrives on the admiration and respect that only a capable leader can command.

Learning to Recognize Signs of Trouble

Building trust and candor is a gradual process, a long chain of positive experiences: trusting employees with important assignments, publicly defending their positions and supporting their ideas, showing candor and fairness in evaluating their work, and so forth. And because trust takes time to build and has natural limits once achieved, it is easy to destroy. Betraying a confidence, breaking a promise, humiliating an employee in public, lying, withholding information, or excluding subordinates from groups in which they feel they rightly belong—any of these can do instant and irreparable damage to a trust relationship that has taken months or years to develop.

Given these limitations, can managers rely on subordinates to come forward with problems before they become critical?

The obvious answer is no, not entirely. Honest, forthright communication is the best source of information about problems that managers have, and good ones make the most of it. At the same time, they learn to recognize subtle signs of danger, and they develop and refine alternative sources of information to fill in the gaps. My interviews indicate that there are several important warning signs that managers can look for.

Decline in information flow is often a first sign of trouble. Streams of information suddenly go dry. Subordinates communicate less, express opinions reluctantly, avoid discussions—even meetings. Reports are late, subordinates are more difficult to reach, and follow-up has to be more thorough and deliberate. In this example, the first warning was a series of glib reassurances that didn't quite jibe with reality:

☐ I was exploration manager for an oil company in Venezuela. I began to notice that when I asked about one particular project, I got very short and superficial answers assuring me that everything was okay. But there were some contradictory signals. For example, labor turnover in the project was quite high. I had a gut feeling that something was seriously wrong. I contacted the area manager, but he couldn't put his finger on any specific problem. I called the field supervisor and still got no clear answers. I went to the field location and spent two days. Nothing. Then I sent a trustworthy young assistant to work with the field crews for a week, and he uncovered the problem. Local labor subcontractors were bribing the workers, increasing turnover, and taking in a lot of money for supplying replacements. We were not only spending more on labor bounties, we were often working with green hands instead of well-trained workers.

Deterioration of morale can reveal itself in lack of enthusiasm, reduced cooperation, increased complaints about workload, a tendency to dump more minor problems on the boss's desk. At a more advanced stage, absenteeism starts to rise and aggressive behavior—increased criticism, irritability, finger pointing, and the like—appears.

Ambiguous verbal messages come from subordinates who aren't quite comfortable with the information they are passing on. They may be reluctant to blow a potential problem out of proportion, or they may be testing to see if the door is open for a more serious discussion.

In one example, the head of an R&D lab asked the woman in charge of a large research project how a newly hired scientist was working out. The woman said, "He's very bright, but a bit strange. But he's working very hard and is extremely enthusiastic. He's okay." The boss missed the message. "I'm glad everything's okay" was all he said.

In this case, the woman's answer was a typical sign of trouble in sandwich form—positive, negative, positive. The subordinate who answers this way may simply be testing her boss's attention. When he failed to pick up on the "he's a bit strange" remark, she dropped the matter. Her boss never found out that she felt threatened by the scientist's brilliance and that his prima donna behavior made her angry. The friction between them grew, and she eventually took a job with another division.

Nonverbal signals can take a wide variety of forms, from body language to social behavior to changes in routines and habits.

The director of the international division of a major U.S. bank noticed that his chief of Asian operations had begun to work with his office door closed during his frequent visits to New York. This was unusual behavior: he was a gregarious soul, always available for lunch or a chat, and a closed door was out of character.

After two or three such visits, the director invited him to lunch to talk business. After a bottle of good wine, the younger man brought up what was really on his mind. He had heard rumors that his name had come up to head the European division—the most prestigious foreign assignment—and that the director had opposed him. The rumors were wrong. In fact, the bank was looking for someone to take the director's job, as he was about to be promoted, and the Asian operations chief was a prime candidate.

Consciously or unconsciously, the man sent a signal by closing his door. The lunch invitation was a nonthreatening way of finding out what the signal meant. At the time this took place, business had not yet begun to suffer, but more serious trouble might have

"It's a hostile attempt to take the company public!"

erupted if this man had continued to brood over false rumors. This prompt response to a nonverbal signal kept a small problem from growing into a big one.

Body language, incidentally, is easily misinterpreted. Popular books have encouraged many people to believe they are experts, but interpreting body language is risky business. Distress signals may be triggered by events in a person's private life, for example, and have nothing to do with the office. A more prudent approach is to see body language merely as an indication of a potential problem, without jumping to conclusions about what the problem may be.

Outside signals, such as customer complaints and problems spotted by other company divisions, are also clear warnings, but they often come too late. By this time, the trouble has usually reached the stage of impaired results—decreasing productivity, deteriorating quality, dwindling orders, declining numbers. By now the manager has long since failed.

Turning Hints into Information

When experienced managers see changes in the behavior of the people they supervise, they do their best to amplify hints and gather supplemental information.

As I pointed out at the beginning of this article, by far the easiest way of obtaining information is to get it from a subordinate, in plain English. Managers who have built good relationships with their subordinates often rely on this method. When they see the early warning signs of trouble, they ask questions.

As I have stressed, the answers to their questions will be only as honest as subordinates want to and dare to give. In other words, successful questioning depends partly on the level of trust. However, it also depends partly on a manager's ability to peel away superficial and sometimes misleading symptoms, much like the outside layers of an onion. Effective managers have good clinical sense. This man, for example, had a gut feeling that he had not yet reached the core of the problem:

☐ My department was responsible for trade with the Far East, and I needed a good manager for China. I found what I thought was the perfect man. He not only knew all the traders but also spoke fluent English, French, Chinese, and Japanese. The new position was a promotion for him in terms of title and meant a big salary increase.

For the first year, he worked hard, things went well, and we made a lot of money. At the same time, he started to complain about his salary, arguing that

other managers reporting to me and doing the same kind of work were getting 20% more—which was true. I told him he'd already had a 25% increase and that if he continued doing well, he could expect further raises over the next couple of years.

Then I began hearing his complaint from third parties all over the Far East. I discussed the matter with him many times, and eventually his salary rose to within 5% of the other managers. But something was still wrong. Then he suddenly got sick and disappeared from the office for two weeks. When he returned, his opening words were about salary.

Over the next couple of months, however, his health continued to deteriorate, and I began to wonder if salary was the real problem after all. I had several long talks with him and finally learned the truth. His deteriorating health was related to the job and the level of responsibility, which was too great for him to handle. He was so anxious that he couldn't sleep and was having problems with his family. As soon as we both understood the cause of his problem, I promised him a different job with less stress and frustration. He immediately became more relaxed and happier with his salary and his life.

The salary issue was only a symptom—a particularly misleading one, since the man was in fact underpaid by comparison with his colleagues. Notice also the escalation of symptoms from complaints to illness and the fact that it took the narrator several discussions to get at the actual truth. His persistence grew from a gut feeling that salary was not the real problem but rather a masking symptom.

> The best, the most common, and the hardest way of getting information is face to face, in plain English.

When conflicts arise between superiors and subordinates, the most common method of punishing the boss is to withhold information. So the greater the conflict is, the less effective direct questioning will be. Furthermore, if an honest answer means pointing out some of the boss's own shortcomings, almost anyone will think twice.

One way of circumventing this difficulty is to design anonymous forms of communication—suggestion boxes, questionnaires, and performance appraisals of managers by the people who work for them.

One manager took advantage of an odd condition in his office space to coax anonymous information from his staff. The offices were on the ninth and tenth floors of an office building and had two elevators of their own, which every employee rode several times a day. The boss put a bulletin board in each of them and posted frequent notices, including a weekly newsletter about office activities, personnel changes, and industry developments. He then let it be known informally that the bulletin boards were open to everyone – no approvals required – and when the first employee notices appeared, he made a point of leaving them in place for a full week. There were only two rules. First, no clippings from newspapers and magazines – contributions had to be original. Second, nothing tasteless or abusive – but complaints and bellyaching were okay.

The bulletin boards flourished, partly because most people had at least an occasional chance to ride alone and post their own views in private. For a while, there was even an anonymous weekly newspaper that handed out praise and criticism pretty

> ## Using information properly is largely a matter of not *misusing* it.

freely and irreverently. It made some people uncomfortable, but it had no more avid reader than the boss, who learned volumes about the problems and views of his staff and organization.

Criticizing the boss's managerial style and professional competence is probably the hardest thing for employees to do. Remember two critical points: First, top performers are the most likely to feel secure enough to criticize, so ask them first. Second, many of your subordinates have learned the hard way that

honest negative feedback can be dangerous. Never ask for it unless you are certain you can handle it.

Building Information Networks

There are big differences between consuming, disseminating, and creating information. Effective managers seem to have a talent for all three.

Using information well is primarily a matter of not *misusing* it – of being discreet about its sources, of using it not as a weapon but only as a means of solving problems and improving the quality of work life.

Spreading information well means not spreading gossip but also not hoarding the truth. People in organizations want – and have a right to – information that will help them do their jobs better or otherwise affect their lives. In general, they also work better and suffer less stress and fewer complications when they are well informed. At the same time – and more important for this discussion – information attracts information. Managers who are generous with what they know seem to get as much as they give.

Creating information, finally, is a question of assembling scattered facts and interpreting them for others. Shaping data in this way is a skill that needs exercise. It is an act of education and, of course, an act of control.

The final positive outcome for information-rich individuals is that information flows to them as well as away from them. This ability to attract, create, and disseminate information can become an immense managerial asset, a self-perpetuating information network, and a means of creating the trust that the upward flow of candid information depends on. ▽

Reprint 89203

Not all corporate success is due to leadership...

In Praise of Followers

by Robert E. Kelley

We are convinced that corporations succeed or fail, compete or crumble, on the basis of how well they are led. So we study great leaders of the past and present and spend vast quantities of time and money looking for leaders to hire and trying to cultivate leadership in the employees we already have.

I have no argument with this enthusiasm. Leaders matter greatly. But in searching so zealously for better leaders we tend to lose sight of the people these leaders will lead. Without his armies, after all, Napoleon was just a man with grandiose ambitions. Organizations stand or fall partly on the basis of how well their leaders lead, but partly also on the basis of how well their followers follow.

In 1987, declining profitability and intensified competition for corporate clients forced a large commercial bank on the east coast to reorganize its operations and cut its work force. Its most seasoned managers had to spend most of their time in the field working with corporate customers. Time and energies were stretched so thin that one department head decided he had no choice but to delegate the responsibility for reorganization to his staff people, who had recently had training in self-management.

Despite grave doubts, the department head set them up as a unit without a leader, responsible to one another and to the bank as a whole for writing their own job descriptions, designing a training program, determining criteria for performance evaluations, planning for operational needs, and helping to achieve overall organizational objectives.

They pulled it off. The bank's officers were delighted and frankly amazed that rank-and-file employees could assume so much responsibility so successfully. In fact, the department's capacity to control and direct itself virtually without leadership saved the organization months of turmoil, and as the bank struggled to remain a major player in its region, valuable management time was freed up to put out other fires.

Robert E. Kelley teaches at the Graduate School of Industrial Administration, Carnegie Mellon University. He is the author of Gold-Collar Worker: Harnessing the Brainpower of the New Work Force *(Addison-Wesley, 1985) and* Consulting: The Complete Guide to a Profitable Career *(Scribner, rev.ed., 1986). The material in this article is drawn from a book in progress,* Followership–Leadership–Partnership. *This is his second article for HBR.*

What was it these singular employees did? Given a goal and parameters, they went where most departments could only have gone under the hands-on guidance of an effective leader. But these employees accepted the delegation of authority and went there alone. They thought for themselves, sharpened their skills, focused their efforts, put on a fine display of grit and spunk and self-control. They followed effectively.

To encourage this kind of effective following in other organizations, we need to understand the nature of the follower's role. To cultivate good followers, we need to understand the human qualities that allow effective followership to occur.

The Role of Follower

Bosses are not necessarily good leaders; subordinates are not necessarily effective followers. Many bosses couldn't lead a horse to water. Many subordinates couldn't follow a parade. Some people avoid either role. Others accept the role thrust upon them and perform it badly.

At different points in their careers, even at different times of the working day, most managers play both roles, though seldom equally well. After all, the leadership role has the glamour and attention. We take courses to learn it, and when we play it well we get applause and recognition. But the reality is that most of us are more often followers than leaders. Even when we have subordinates, we still have bosses. For every committee we chair, we sit as a member on several others.

So followership dominates our lives and organizations, but not our thinking, because our preoccupation with leadership keeps us from considering the nature and the importance of the follower.

What distinguishes an effective from an ineffective follower is enthusiastic, intelligent, and self-reliant participation—without star billing—in the pursuit of an organizational goal. Effective followers differ in their motivations for following and in their perceptions of the role. Some choose followership as their primary role at work and serve as team players who take satisfaction in helping to further a cause, an idea, a product, a service, or, more rarely, a person. Others are leaders in some situations but choose the follower role in a particular context. Both these groups view the role of follower as legitimate, inherently valuable, even virtuous.

Some potentially effective followers derive motivation from ambition. By proving themselves in the follower's role, they hope to win the confidence of peers and superiors and move up the corporate ladder. These people do not see followership as attractive in itself. All the same, they can become good followers if they accept the value of learning the role, studying leaders from a subordinate's perspective, and polishing the followership skills that will always stand them in good stead.

Understanding motivations and perceptions is not enough, however. Since followers with different motivations can perform equally well, I examined the behavior that leads to effective and less effective following among people committed to the organization and came up with two underlying behavioral dimensions that help to explain the difference.

One dimension measures to what degree followers exercise independent, critical thinking. The other ranks them on a passive/active scale. The resulting diagram identifies five followership patterns.

Sheep are passive and uncritical, lacking in initiative and sense of responsibility. They perform the tasks given them and stop. Yes People are a livelier but equally unenterprising group. Dependent on a leader for inspiration, they can be aggressively deferential, even servile. Bosses weak in judgment and self-confidence tend to like them and to form alliances with them that can stultify the organization.

Alienated Followers are critical and independent in their thinking but passive in carrying out their role. Somehow, sometime, something turned them off. Often cynical, they tend to sink gradually into disgruntled acquiescence, seldom openly opposing a leader's efforts. In the very center of the diagram we have Survivors, who perpetually sample the wind and live by the slogan "better safe than sorry." They are adept at surviving change.

In the upper right-hand corner, finally, we have Effective Followers, who think for themselves and carry out their duties and assignments with energy and assertiveness. Because they are risk takers, self-

starters, and independent problem solvers, they get consistently high ratings from peers and many superiors. Followership of this kind can be a positive and acceptable choice for parts or all of our lives—a source of pride and fulfillment.

Effective followers are well-balanced and responsible adults who can succeed without strong leadership. Many followers believe they offer as much value to the organization as leaders do, especially in project or task-force situations. In an organization of effective followers, a leader tends to be more an overseer of change and progress than a hero. As organizational structures flatten, the quality of those who follow will become more and more important. As Chester I. Barnard wrote 50 years ago in *The Functions of the Executive*, "The decision as to whether an order has authority or not lies with the person to whom it is addressed, and does not reside in 'persons of authority' or those who issue orders."

The Qualities of Followers

Effective followers share a number of essential qualities:

1. They manage themselves well.
2. They are committed to the organization and to a purpose, principle, or person outside themselves.
3. They build their competence and focus their efforts for maximum impact.
4. They are courageous, honest, and credible.

Self-Management. Paradoxically, the key to being an effective follower is the ability to think for oneself—to exercise control and independence and to work without close supervision. Good followers are people to whom a leader can safely delegate responsibility, people who anticipate needs at their own level of competence and authority.

Another aspect of this paradox is that effective followers see themselves—except in terms of line responsibility—as the equals of the leaders they follow. They are more apt to openly and unapologetically disagree with leadership and less likely to be intimidated by hierarchy and organizational structure. At the same time, they can see that the people they follow are, in turn, following the lead of others, and they try to appreciate the goals and needs of the team and the organization. Ineffective followers, on the other hand, buy into the hierarchy and, seeing themselves as subservient, vacillate between despair over their seeming powerlessness and attempts to manipulate leaders for their own purposes. Either their fear of powerlessness becomes a self-fulfilling

prophecy—for themselves and often for their work units as well—or their resentment leads them to undermine the team's goals.

Self-managed followers give their organizations a significant cost advantage because they eliminate much of the need for elaborate supervisory control systems that, in any case, often lower morale. In 1985, a large midwestern bank redesigned its personnel selection system to attract self-managed workers. Those conducting interviews began to look for particular types of experience and capacities—initiative, teamwork, independent thinking of all kinds—and the bank revamped its orientation program to emphasize self-management. At the executive level, role playing was introduced into the interview process: how you disagree with your boss, how you prioritize your in-basket after a vacation. In the three years since, employee turnover has dropped dramatically, the need for supervisors has decreased, and administrative costs have gone down.

Of course not all leaders and managers like having self-managing subordinates. Some would rather have sheep or yes people. The best that good followers can do in this situation is to protect themselves with a little career self-management—that is, to stay attractive in the marketplace. The qualities that make a good follower are too much in demand to go begging for long.

Commitment. Effective followers are committed to something—a cause, a product, an organization, an idea—in addition to the care of their own lives and careers. Some leaders misinterpret this commitment. Seeing their authority acknowledged, they mistake loyalty to a goal for loyalty to themselves. But the fact is that many effective followers see leaders merely as coadventurers on a worthy crusade, and if they suspect their leader of flagging commitment or

> Self-confident followers
> see colleagues as allies and
> leaders as equals.

conflicting motives they may just withdraw their support, either by changing jobs or by contriving to change leaders.

The opportunities and the dangers posed by this kind of commitment are not hard to see. On the one hand, commitment is contagious. Most people like working with colleagues whose hearts are in their work. Morale stays high. Workers who begin to wander from their purpose are jostled back into line. Projects stay on track and on time. In addition, an ap-

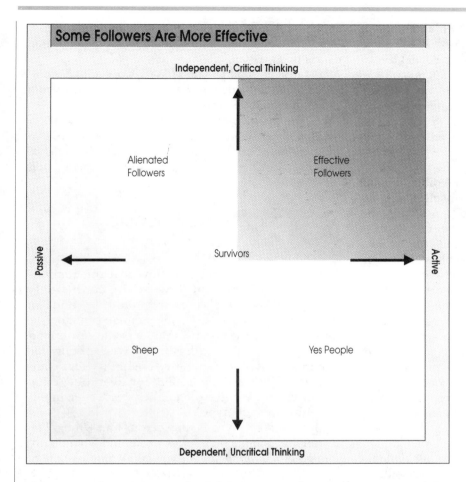

Some Followers Are More Effective

Independent, Critical Thinking

Alienated Followers

Effective Followers

Passive

Survivors

Active

Sheep

Yes People

Dependent, Uncritical Thinking

preciation of commitment and the way it works can give managers an extra tool with which to understand and channel the energies and loyalties of their subordinates.

On the other hand, followers who are strongly committed to goals not consistent with the goals of their companies can produce destructive results. Leaders having such followers can even lose control of their organizations.

A scientist at a computer company cared deeply about making computer technology available to the masses, and her work was outstanding. Since her goal was in line with the company's goals, she had few problems with top management. Yet she saw her department leaders essentially as facilitators of her dream, and when managers worked at cross-purposes to that vision, she exercised all of her considerable political skills to their detriment. Her immediate supervisors saw her as a thorn in the side, but she was quite effective in furthering her cause because she saw eye to eye with company leaders. But what if her vision and the company's vision had differed?

Effective followers temper their loyalties to satisfy organizational needs—or they find new organizations. Effective leaders know how to channel the energies of strong commitment in ways that will satisfy corporate goals as well as a follower's personal needs.

Competence and Focus. On the grounds that committed incompetence is still incompetence, effective followers master skills that will be useful to their organizations. They generally hold higher performance standards than the work environment requires, and continuing education is second nature to them, a staple in their professional development.

Less effective followers expect training and development to come to them. The only education they acquire is force-fed. If not sent to a seminar, they don't go. Their competence deteriorates unless some leader gives them parental care and attention.

Good followers take on extra work gladly, but first they do a superb job on their core responsibilities. They are good judges of their own strengths and weaknesses, and they contribute well to teams. Asked to perform in areas where they are poorly qualified, they speak up. Like athletes stretching their capacities, they don't mind chancing failure if they know they can succeed, but they are careful to spare the company wasted energy, lost time, and poor performance by accepting challenges that coworkers are better prepared to meet. Good followers see coworkers as colleagues rather than competitors.

At the same time, effective followers often search for overlooked problems. A woman on a new product development team discovered that no one was responsible for coordinating engineering, marketing, and manufacturing. She worked out an interdepartmental review schedule that identified the people who should be involved at each stage of development. Instead of burdening her boss with yet another problem, this woman took the initiative to present the issue along with a solution.

Another woman I interviewed described her efforts to fill a dangerous void in the company she cared about. Young managerial talent in this manufacturing corporation had traditionally made careers in production. Convinced that foreign competition would alter the shape of the industry, she realized that marketing was a neglected area. She took classes, attended seminars, and read widely. More important, she visited customers to get feedback about her company's and competitors' products, and she soon knew more about the product's customer appeal and market position than any of her peers. The extra competence did wonders for her own career, but it also helped her company weather a storm it had not seen coming.

Courage. Effective followers are credible, honest, and courageous. They establish themselves as independent, critical thinkers whose knowledge and judgment can be trusted. They give credit where credit is due, admitting mistakes and sharing successes. They form their own views and ethical standards and stand up for what they believe in.

Insightful, candid, and fearless, they can keep leaders and colleagues honest and informed. The other side of the coin of course is that they can also cause great trouble for a leader with questionable ethics.

Jerome LiCari, the former R&D director at Beech-Nut, suspected for several years that the apple concentrate Beech-Nut was buying from a new supplier at 20% below market price was adulterated. His department suggested switching suppliers, but top management at the financially strapped company put the burden of proof on R&D.

By 1981, LiCari had accumulated strong evidence of adulteration and issued a memo recommending a change of supplier. When he got no response, he went

> **Courageous followers can keep a leader honest – and out of trouble.**

to see his boss, the head of operations. According to LiCari, he was threatened with dismissal for lack of team spirit. LiCari then went to the president of Beech-Nut, and when that, too, produced no results, he gave up his three-year good-soldier effort, followed his conscience, and resigned. His last performance evaluation praised his expertise and loyalty, but said his judgment was "colored by naiveté and impractical ideals."

In 1986, Beech-Nut and LiCari's two bosses were indicted on several hundred counts of conspiracy to commit fraud by distributing adulterated apple juice. In November 1987, the company pleaded guilty and agreed to a fine of $2 million. In February of this year, the two executives were found guilty on a majority of the charges. The episode cost Beech-Nut an estimated $25 million and a 20% loss of market share.

Asked during the trial if he had been naive, LiCari said, "I guess I was. I thought apple juice should be made from apples."

Is LiCari a good follower? Well, no, not to his dishonest bosses. But yes, he is almost certainly the kind of employee most companies want to have: loyal, honest, candid with his superiors, and thoroughly credible. In an ethical company involved unintentionally in questionable practices, this kind of follower can head off embarrassment, expense, and litigation.

Cultivating Effective Followers

You may have noticed by now that the qualities that make effective followers are, confusingly enough, pretty much the same qualities found in some effective leaders. This is no mere coincidence, of course. But the confusion underscores an important point. If a person has initiative, self-control, commitment, talent, honesty, credibility, and courage, we say, "Here is a leader!" By definition, a follower cannot exhibit the qualities of leadership. It violates our stereotype.

But our stereotype is ungenerous and wrong. Followership is not a person but a role, and what distinguishes followers from leaders is not intelligence or character but the role they play. As I pointed out at the beginning of this article, effective followers and effective leaders are often the same people playing different parts at different hours of the day.

In many companies, the leadership track is the only road to career success. In almost all companies, leadership is taught and encouraged while followership is not. Yet effective followership is a prerequisite for organizational success. Your organization can take four steps to cultivate effective followers in your work force.

1. *Redefining Followership and Leadership.* Our stereotyped but unarticulated definitions of leadership and followership shape our expectations when we occupy either position. If a leader is defined as responsible for motivating followers, he or she will likely act toward followers as if they needed motivation. If we agree that a leader's job is to transform followers, then it must be a follower's job to provide the clay. If followers fail to need transformation, the leader looks ineffective. The way we define the roles clearly influences the outcome of the interaction.

Instead of seeing the leadership role as superior to and more active than the role of the follower, we can think of them as equal but different activities. The operative definitions are roughly these: people who are effective in the leader role have the vision to set corporate goals and strategies, the interpersonal skills to achieve consensus, the verbal capacity to communicate enthusiasm to large and diverse groups of individuals, the organizational talent to coordinate disparate efforts, and, above all, the desire to lead.

People who are effective in the follower role have the vision to see both the forest and the trees, the social capacity to work well with others, the strength of character to flourish without heroic status, the moral and psychological balance to pursue personal and corporate goals at no cost to either, and, above all, the desire to participate in a team effort for the accomplishment of some greater common purpose.

This view of leadership and followership can be conveyed to employees directly and indirectly—in training and by example. The qualities that make good followers and the value the company places on effective followership can be articulated in explicit follower training. Perhaps the best way to convey this message, however, is by example. Since each of us plays a follower's part at least from time to time, it is essential that we play it well, that we contribute our

competence to the achievement of team goals, that we support the team leader with candor and self-control, that we do our best to appreciate and enjoy the role of quiet contribution to a larger, common cause.

2. *Honing Followership Skills.* Most organizations assume that leadership has to be taught but that everyone knows how to follow. This assumption is

> **Good leaders know how to follow—and they set an example for others.**

based on three faulty premises: (1) that leaders are more important than followers, (2) that following is simply doing what you are told to do, and (3) that followers inevitably draw their energy and aims, even their talent, from the leader. A program of follower training can correct this misapprehension by focusing on topics like:

Improving independent, critical thinking.
Self-management.
    Disagreeing agreeably.
    Building credibility.
    Aligning personal and organizational goals and commitments.
    Acting responsibly toward the organization, the leader, coworkers, and oneself.
    Similarities and differences between leadership and followership roles.
    Moving between the two roles with ease.

3. *Performance Evaluation and Feedback.* Most performance evaluations include a section on leadership skills. Followership evaluation would include items like the ones I have discussed. Instead of rating employees on leadership qualities such as self-management, independent thinking, originality, courage, competence, and credibility, we can rate them on these same qualities in both the leadership and followership roles and then evaluate each individual's ability to shift easily from the one role to the other. A variety of performance perspectives will help most people understand better how well they play their various organizational roles.

Moreover, evaluations can come from peers, subordinates, and self as well as from supervisors. The process is simple enough: peers and subordinates who come into regular or significant contact with another employee fill in brief, periodic questionnaires where they

rate the individual on followership qualities. Findings are then summarized and given to the employee being rated.

4. *Organizational Structures That Encourage Followership.* Unless the value of good following is somehow built into the fabric of the organization, it is likely to remain a pleasant conceit to which everyone pays occasional lip service but no dues.

Groups with many leaders can be chaos. Groups with none can be very productive.

Here are four good ways to incorporate the concept into your corporate culture:

In leaderless groups, all members assume equal responsibility for achieving goals. These are usually small task forces of people who can work together under their own supervision. However hard it is to imagine a group with more than one leader, groups with none at all can be highly productive if their members have the qualities of effective followers.

Groups with temporary and rotating leadership are another possibility. Again, such groups are probably best kept small and the rotation fairly frequent, although the notion might certainly be extended to include the administration of a small department for, say, six-month terms. Some of these temporary leaders will be less effective than others, of course, and some may be weak indeed, which is why critics maintain that this structure is inefficient. Why not let the best leader lead? Why suffer through the tenure of less effective leaders? There are two reasons. First, experience of the leadership role is essential to the education of effective followers. Second, followers learn that they must compensate for ineffective leadership by exercising their skill as good followers. Rotating leader or not, they are bound to be

faced with ineffective leadership more than once in their careers.

Delegation to the lowest level is a third technique for cultivating good followers. Nordstrom's, the Seattle-based department store chain, gives each sales clerk responsibility for servicing and satisfying the customer, including the authority to make refunds without supervisory approval. This kind of delegation makes even people at the lowest levels responsible for their own decisions and for thinking independently about their work.

Finally, companies can use rewards to underline the importance of good followership. This is not as easy as it sounds. Managers dependent on yes people and sheep for ego gratification will not leap at the idea of extra rewards for the people who make them most uncomfortable. In my research, I have found that effective followers get mixed treatment. About half the time, their contributions lead to substantial rewards. The other half of the time they are punished by their superiors for exercising judgment, taking risks, and failing to conform. Many managers insist that they want independent subordinates who can think for themselves. In practice, followers who challenge their bosses run the risk of getting fired.

In today's flatter, leaner organization, companies will not succeed without the kind of people who take pride and satisfaction in the role of supporting player, doing the less glorious work without fanfare. Organizations that want the benefits of effective followers must find ways of rewarding them, ways of bringing them into full partnership in the enterprise. Think of the thousands of companies that achieve adequate performance and lackluster profits with employees they treat like second-class citizens. Then imagine for a moment the power of an organization blessed with fully engaged, fully energized, fully appreciated followers.

Author's note: I am indebted to Pat Chew for her contributions to this article. I also want to thank Janet Nordin, Howard Seckler, Paul Brophy, Stuart Mechlin, Ellen Mechlin, and Syed Shariq for their critical input.

Reprint 88606

The Middle Manager
and Power

Fernando Bartolomé and André Laurent

The manager: master and servant of power

Most managers are action oriented. As a result, many are not inclined to be introspective about how they relate to others on the job. They don't fully realize, for example, how power differences can disturb interpersonal relations at work and, consequently, undermine organizational effectiveness.

> *"Conflicts arise because managers don't understand the effects of power on behavior."*

Let's look at three typical problems:

☐ Brian Dolan and John Miller, both senior engineers in an electronics company, had worked well as colleagues in their company's R&D department. Their relationship was friendly and informal. Each felt free to drop in unannounced on the other to discuss technical problems or swap company gossip.

Then Brian was promoted to director of R&D, and shortly thereafter he called John and asked him to come to his office to discuss installation plans for the company's new computer-aided design system. The call puzzled and angered John. Brian was only two doors away. Why didn't he just drop by? After all, they were good friends. Why did he have to play the boss? When John went to Brian's office, it was all he could do to hide his irritation. Brian greeted him warmly, but John was reserved during their discussion.

Why, Brian wondered on the trip home that evening, had John acted so oddly? Was it because he had been promoted and not John? That had to be it. John was jealous. John, on the other hand, didn't understand how Brian's new position could make him insensitive to how John might react.

☐ Mary Scarpa, divisional director for a specialty steel fabricator, asked Roger Harrison, a middle manager, for his opinion on a major capital investment decision she was about to make. Roger had serious reservations about the assumptions underlying her cash flow projections. He wanted to level with her, but he also worried that honest criticism would upset her. He knew Mary could be very touchy. Although she had asked for candid feedback, Roger wasn't sure she really meant it; he sensed she really wanted reinforcement. Feeling caught in a bind, Roger conveniently "forgot" her request.

Annoyed by Roger's behavior, Mary complained to a colleague at another company about problems with her subordinates, saying they just wouldn't stick their necks out. They were afraid to give honest opinions because they were insecure, she said. On his part, Roger was insensitive to the reasons why bosses may find it risky to have subordinates challenge their judgment, even when they ask for it.

☐ Dick Rapp, vice president of production for a household appliance manufacturer, told his subordinates that his priority was quality control and cost containment. He wanted defect and scrap rates brought down. He wanted the division to be results driven, not rule driven. "If you have to bend a rule to get the job done, do it," Rapp would say.

His employees took him at his word at first and assumed that any improvement in efficiency would be welcome. But they quickly learned otherwise. Dick Rapp cared as much about style and form as he did about substance. How memos were worded and typed, for example, seemed to concern him as much as what they said. He also chewed out several plant supervisors for approving ad hoc scheduling and other changes and not going through the chain of command.

Understandably, this behavior frustrated Dick's subordinates. They faced conflicting expecta-

Mr. Bartolomé is associate professor of management at Bentley College in Waltham, Massachusetts. He is also visiting lecturer at INSEAD, the European Institute of Business Administration in Fontainebleau, France, and at the Oxford Centre for Management Studies.

Mr. Laurent is professor of organizational behavior at INSEAD, where he is doing comparative, cross-cultural management and organizational research.

tions, and they had to take time away from important tasks to meet what they considered frivolous demands. No one tried to understand, though, why bosses prefer to have things done their way and how this may be their means of heightening their feelings of being in control and reducing uncertainty. And nobody dared to explore these issues with Dick, nor could he see that he was sending mixed messages and burying people in the very red tape he wanted them to cut through.

How did these situations develop? Did Brian Dolan subconsciously need to pull rank on subordinates? Did Mary Scarpa relish putting her employees in a double bind? Did Dick Rapp enjoy tripping up his people? Were the subordinates rebellious people, unwilling to accept authority and take direction?

Such problems occur with surprising frequency in work situations. Usually they arise not because superiors are inherently insensitive or power hungry or because subordinates are naturally rebellious but because people don't understand how strongly hierarchical position affects behavior in organizations. Workplace conflicts are often attributed to personality differences, but the root of the problem is usually structural. The organization's power hierarchy can distort mutual expectations.

"Attention, all department heads! The buck stops there. I've had it!"

Power in the organization

Unevenness of power in the organization subtly influences how managers and subordinates relate to each other. Mary couldn't understand Roger's reticence. But if she had reflected on her own experiences as a subordinate, she might have realized that she too had been cautious at times about giving honest feedback to superiors. Had Brian been able to put himself in John's shoes and think of a new R&D director officiously summoning *him*, he might have better understood John's behavior.

Dick was a results-driven manager who said he cared about quality, not style. Today he works for superiors whose preference for ritualistic, by-the-book action frustrates him. Yet he can't see that he's doing the same thing. He doesn't relate his own experience as a subordinate to the feelings and behavior of the people working for him.

Brian, Mary, and Dick all had trouble putting themselves in their subordinates' shoes. In subordinate roles, on the other hand, John and Roger couldn't see how it might feel to be a boss. This lack of sensitivity on both sides can have ripple effects throughout the organization. Managers who believe

they are on the receiving end of unreasonable or unfair actions from their bosses, for example, may act similarly toward those below them in the organizational pyramid. And the pattern may repeat itself down the chain of command. Or relations with peers may suffer. A troubled relationship at one level can affect many other relationships.

When superiors can't see how their behavior affects their subordinates, their authority may also deteriorate. Most bosses know instinctively that their power depends more on employees' compliance than on threats or sanctions. When managers create no-win situations for people, as Mary did, or make confusing demands on workers, as did Dick, subordinates may respond by losing enthusiasm or withdrawing commitment. If workers think they've been put in impossible situations or if a superior's exaggerated need for power makes them feel inferior, they may give the company their worst rather than their best. The response could mean just going through the motions of the job or even sabotaging organizational goals.

True, managers have power. They can call on official sanctions for punishing uncooperative subordinates. But such blatant use of their clout is rarely able to restore effective working relationships. It is a weak rather than a strong pillar of authority.

There are other consequences arising from this asymmetry in power relations and role perceptions, as we can see when we look at managers as subordinates. If the danger for superiors is being insufficiently sensitive about their subordinates' potential reactions, the danger for subordinates tends to be excessive concern about superiors' potential reactions.

Managers who worry excessively about offending their bosses are much less likely to defend subordinates when higher-ups deal unfairly with them.

But if a manager doesn't defend subordinates, he or she will lose their respect. When subordinates sense that the boss won't defend them against unfairness, their morale will plummet and they will withdraw commitment to the job. A vicious circle results. As their performance deteriorates, their superior's position weakens further. The boss will receive fewer rewards and resources to dispense to subordinates, thus further undermining his or her effectiveness as distinct from merely titular authority.

It's ironic that so many managers are insensitive to this problem because almost all managers occupy a dual position in the organization. They have subordinates who report to them, and they report to superiors. Being both masters and servants of power, they should be able to understand the perspectives of the two groups of people who play the most important roles in their professional lives—namely, their superiors and subordinates.

To probe this duality of the manager's role and the sharp differences in expectations that power differences create, we recently collected questionnaires from 105 executives of major companies. We divided the people into two similar groups, matched according to age, management position, and other characteristics. We asked one group of managers to describe the expectations they had for their superiors, the second, to describe expectations for subordinates. In addition, we had conversations with a number of the executives we surveyed.

As the *Exhibit* shows, the expectations of the two groups differed sharply. Of the managers we asked to take the superior role, 78% said they are primarily concerned about subordinates' performance. A majority also said they expect subordinates to be loyal and honest. A typical comment was "I expect effective performance and loyalty even when difficult or unpleasant duties have to be performed."

The superiors we talked to view loyalty, honesty, and performance as linked. They also see honest communication and a willingness to follow orders as necessary to get the job done. But at the same time, they don't see the potential conflict that lies in demanding loyalty and desiring honesty and frankness from subordinates. Many seem unaware of the extent to which they confuse loyalty with agreement and obedience. They also seem to underestimate the difficulty subordinates have in being honest about their own problems or weaknesses with people who have so much influence on their careers.

What happens when the shoe is on the other foot?

When managers take the subordinate position, they expect leadership and good communica-

Exhibit	Comparison of role expectations	
	Desired traits	**Percentage of managers who mentioned this trait** Multiple choices were possible
What managers expect from subordinates	Good task performance	78 %
	Loyalty and obedience	60
	Honesty	53
	Initiative	31
	Other skills	26
What managers expect from superiors	Good communication and feedback	64 %
	Leadership	60
	Encouragement and support	50
	Delegation and autonomy	37
	Professional competence	21
	Information	17

tion from their superiors. A director of finance we talked to said, "I expect my superior to give me clear messages about what he expects from me." A vice president of engineering commented, "The boss should establish his requirements absolutely clearly."

Why do subordinates want clear communication and decisive leadership from their superiors? One reason is that they need reassurance that their bosses are competent. Clear communication is a good measure of competence. Subordinates also want to minimize uncertainty in their environment. Clear communication reduces guesswork. But decisiveness and clarity of communication alone aren't enough. Our interviews revealed that subordinates also want consistency.

Managers in both interview groups gave initiative and autonomy much lower ratings than we had expected. Fewer than a third of the people who took the superior role said they expect initiative from subordinates. Only 37% of those in the subordinate position said it is important for their superiors to grant them autonomy. This is odd when one considers how strongly management experts today endorse job autonomy and broad participation in decision making.

Subordinates don't want superiors to be constantly peering over their shoulders. Instead, they want enough leeway to do the jobs as they see fit. "The boss shouldn't interfere in details," a sales manager said, and "My manager should give me enough space to do my job," said an administrative officer.

Subordinates also want fair performance appraisals, support, and encouragement. Another sales manager said, "My superior should show fairness, objectivity, honesty, and a willingness to give feedback without my having to ask for it." A division manager answered, "I expect help, encouragement, and coaching, and the opportunity to learn from my mistakes." And an R&D director reported, "I expect support in conflict situations."

Managers as superiors

As bosses, managers are not only often unaware of how they misuse their power in relation to subordinates, but they are also frequently unaware of the contradictory messages they send and their motives for doing so. For example, they may tell subordinates that they expect them to be candid and to feel free to offer criticism. Yet at the same time, they communicate disapproval of candid feedback through subtle and sometimes not so subtle cues.

Managers may even confuse excessive deference (pleasing behavior) with the normal level of compliance that they feel they have a legitimate right to expect. They may not see the ways in which they signal to subordinates demands for excessively deferential behavior—and they are also often unaware of the deep resentment that these demands produce.

In the superior role, most managers say that they are more concerned about their subordinates' performance than with obedience for its own sake or with workers doing things the boss's way. Despite the overt message they send, however—"good performance is what really counts in my department"—many managers communicate subtly to subordinates that obedience and deference are just as important, if not more so. This is usually subconscious on the managers' part.

Most executives have trouble learning about the expectations their subordinates have of them simply because they are rarely forthright about how they'd like *their* bosses to behave. Actually, most subordinates work hard to adapt their behavior to what they think the boss expects. Although the chief's actions may be very frustrating to them, few will express openly their dislike of the behavior or try to persuade the boss to change—even when invited to criticize.

This reticence can lead to surprising angry outbursts when smoldering resentment suddenly surfaces. The superior ends up wondering, "Why didn't you come to me earlier with this problem?" Bosses will often deny blame and claim they've always had an open-door policy. Many apparently assume that such a policy alone is sufficient to guarantee a fully open relationship and to minimize the effects of power.

Managers as subordinates

As subordinates, managers develop an exaggerated concern over pleasing their bosses because they believe they have very little power to change the superior's behavior. Whatever the boss's rhetoric may be, they are convinced they know the real score. As a result, they spend much time scrutinizing the boss's behavior for cues that indicate approval or disapproval.

As one manager put it, "I suppose it's true: I study [my manager's] likes, dislikes, and other personal tastes; his objectives and motivations and the time pressure he may be under." One division head said of his superior, "I take into account how his thinking differs from mine, what things he is likely to view in a different way."

> *"Managers must look for subtle cues. If they do, they can create the necessary atmosphere of trust for solving problems. But they can't do it instantly."*

Managers as superiors know how much they depend on their subordinates' performance and, therefore, how much real power, as opposed to formal power, their subordinates have over them. But when bosses are subordinates, they often forget this reality of organizational life. They forget that the boss's performance depends heavily on how committed the subordinates are to their jobs and on the quality of their work. Consequently, the subordinates often seem to focus too much on accommodating their superiors' stylistic preferences and not enough on performance per se. They don't always recognize that they possess real power that they can use with their bosses to negotiate and obtain satisfaction for their legitimate needs and demands. They seem unable to transfer their experiences as bosses to their behavior as subordinates.

Because subordinates perceive themselves as being too weak to alter their superiors' behavior, managers in the subordinate role are extremely concerned with whether they have a natural match ("good chemistry") with their bosses. When relating to subordinates, on the other hand, managers don't seem concerned about compatibility. They assume that their subordinates can easily learn to conform to their expectations and that this reshaping of behavior will not harm the organization. In reality, however, having to adapt like this is likely to keep subordinates from making a full contribution. In most cases, inhibiting people this way creates resentment.

Consequences of power

When managers fail to understand how deeply the unequal distribution of power can hurt interpersonal relations and productivity, serious problems can arise for the organization. The most important and pervasive negative effect of the hierarchical structure can be summarized in the saying, "Trust flees authority." Good ideas often remain unexpressed because subordinates believe they will be punished for disagreeing with their superiors or showing too much competence. Honest feedback about the superior's managerial style is withheld because subordinates are afraid they'll be blackballed when decisions on promotions are made.

Reducing the upward flow of ideas and feedback can have many adverse consequences. Take, for example, the many MBO programs that run into difficulty. An honest contract between superiors and subordinates, based on a fair exchange of contributions and rewards between the individuals and the organization, should be at the core of an MBO program. This is only possible, however, if subordinates feel that they will not be punished for defending their interests or balking at unreasonable demands from the top. Unfair MBO agreements may work in the short term, but they will usually fail in the long haul.

When managers are dissatisfied with the contracts they have with their bosses, unfair contracts may follow at each level down the ladder. Such a pattern can damage management's credibility as well as the whole organization's authority.

What can managers do?

Nobody is to blame for these distortions of hierarchical power. The problem is inherent in organizational life because authority differences are both inevitable and also functional to a degree. The problem cannot be avoided, but it can be controlled if managers strive to link their two roles as masters and servants of power.

When they are in the superior role, they should ask themselves, "How would I feel if my boss behaved this way or demanded this of me?" For example, Brian in our first case might have stopped to think, "I need to talk to John, but if I summon him, he may think I'm trying to remind him that I got the promotion and he didn't. And why, after all, am I doing this? Can't I get the information just as well by phone? Come to think of it, I remember the time I got angry when *my* boss asked me to come running on a moment's notice."

Managers can also ask whether the tasks they assign to subordinates are truly critical to the job—as distinct from ritualistic demands motivated by an unconscious desire to show people that "rank has its privileges" or to reassure themselves that they can make people do what they want them to do. "Power: use it or lose it," as another saying goes.

The burden for getting relationships back on a healthy basis falls mainly to bosses because they have more power and because it would be unrealistic to expect subordinates to take the initiative and complain about their bosses' unreasonable or unfair conduct. Even if superiors encourage honest feedback, people rarely believe that they mean it. So, generally they won't risk testing the boss's sincerity.

When they are the superior, managers need to ask themselves, "What can I do to increase my employees' trust, or at least decrease their mistrust? What signals may indicate problems?" Managers need to learn to monitor subordinates' subtle cues. It helps to understand that it's easier for subordinates to learn about bosses' reactions and desires because superiors are more likely to express their feelings openly. By the same token, it's more difficult for bosses to find out their subordinates' real feelings; they're likely to express them indirectly and with caution.

Directly questioning subordinates rarely works when you're trying to find out what's wrong. Managers must look for subtle cues. Eventually, they can create the necessary atmosphere of trust for solving problems, but they can't do it instantly. It will come only from consistently demonstrating fairness and honesty toward the people working for them.

In the subordinate role, on the other hand, managers may find that they can more easily manage their relationships with superiors by just asking them what they want. This approach should work with competent and insightful superiors. But for some people, asking questions may not be enough; observing behavior is often equally important. Once again, the managerial subordinate should take advantage of his or her own experience as a boss and ask, "What do I care most about when I'm in the superior role?" Managers who can answer this question insightfully and realistically should be able to move ahead in the important process of understanding and managing their own superiors. ▽

Reprint 86603

Power failure in management circuits

Rosabeth Moss Kanter

The position, not the person, often determines whether a manager has power

When one thinks of "power," one often assumes that a person is the source of it and that some mystical charismatic element is at work. Of course, with some people this is undoubtedly so; they derive power from how other people perceive them. In organizations, however—says this author—power is not so much a question of people but of positions. Drawing a distinction between productive and oppressive power, the author maintains that the former is a function of having open channels to supplies, support, and information; the latter is a function of these channels being closed. She then describes three positions that are classically powerless: first-line supervisors, staff professionals, and, surprisingly, chief executive officers. These positions can be powerless because of difficulties in maintaining open lines of information and sup-

port. Seeing powerlessness in these positions as dangerous for organizations, she urges managers to restructure and redesign their organizations in order to eliminate pockets of powerlessness.

Ms. Kanter is professor of sociology and organization and management at Yale University, where she conducts research on organization design and change processes. She is the author of *Men and Women of the Corporation* (New York: Basic Books, 1977) and numerous other articles and books on life in today's organizations.

Power is America's last dirty word. It is easier to talk about money—and much easier to talk about sex—than it is to talk about power. People who have it deny it; people who want it do not want to appear to hunger for it; and people who engage in its machinations do so secretly.

Yet, because it turns out to be a critical element in effective managerial behavior, power should come out from undercover. Having searched for years for those styles or skills that would identify capable organization leaders, many analysts, like myself, are rejecting individual traits or situational appropriateness as key and finding the sources of a leader's real power.

Access to resources and information and the ability to act quickly make it possible to accomplish more and to pass on more resources and information to subordinates. For this reason, people tend to prefer bosses with "clout." When employees perceive their manager as influential upward and outward, their status is enhanced by association and they generally have high morale and feel less critical or resistant to their boss.[1] More powerful leaders are also more likely to delegate (they are too busy to do it all themselves), to reward talent, and to build a team that places subordinates in significant positions.

Powerlessness, in contrast, tends to breed bossiness rather than true leadership. In large organizations, at least, it is powerlessness that often creates ineffective, desultory management and petty, dictatorial, rules-minded managerial styles. Account-

1. Donald C. Pelz, "Influence: A Key to Effective Leadership in the First-Line Supervisor," *Personnel*, November 1952, p. 209.

ability without power—responsibility for results without the resources to get them—creates frustration and failure. People who see themselves as weak and powerless and find their subordinates resisting or discounting them tend to use more punishing forms of influence. If organizational power can "ennoble," then, recent research shows, organizational powerlessness can (with apologies to Lord Acton) "corrupt." [2]

So perhaps power, in the organization at least, does not deserve such a bad reputation. Rather than connoting only dominance, control, and oppression, *power* can mean efficacy and capacity—something managers and executives need to move the organization toward its goals. Power in organizations is analogous in simple terms to physical power: it is the ability to mobilize resources (human and material) to get things done. The true sign of power, then, is accomplishment—not fear, terror, or tyranny. Where the power is "on," the system can be productive; where the power is "off," the system bogs down.

But saying that people need power to be effective in organizations does not tell us where it comes from or why some people, in some jobs, systematically seem to have more of it than others. In this article I want to show that to discover the sources of productive power, we have to look not at the *person*—as conventional classifications of effective managers and employees do—but at the *position* the person occupies in the organization.

Where does power come from?

The effectiveness that power brings evolves from two kinds of capacities: first, access to the resources, information, and support necessary to carry out a task; and, second, ability to get cooperation in doing what is necessary. (*Exhibit I* identifies some symbols of an individual manager's power.)

Both capacities derive not so much from a leader's style and skill as from his or her location in the formal and informal systems of the organization—in both job definition and connection to other important people in the company. Even the ability to get cooperation from subordinates is strongly defined by the manager's clout outward. People are more responsive to bosses who look as if they can get more for them from the organization.

We can regard the uniquely organizational sources of power as consisting of three "lines":

1. *Lines of supply.* Influence outward, over the environment, means that managers have the capacity to bring in the things that their own organizational domain needs—materials, money, resources to distribute as rewards, and perhaps even prestige.

2. *Lines of information.* To be effective, managers need to be "in the know" in both the formal and the informal sense.

3. *Lines of support.* In a formal framework, a manager's job parameters need to allow for nonordinary action, for a show of discretion or exercise of judgment. Thus managers need to know that they can assume innovative, risk-taking activities without having to go through the stifling multilayered approval process. And, informally, managers need the backing of other important figures in the organization whose tacit approval becomes another resource they bring to their own work unit as well as a sign of the manager's being "in."

Note that productive power has to do with *connections* with other parts of a system. Such systemic aspects of power derive from two sources—job activities and political alliances:

1. Power is most easily accumulated when one has a job that is designed and located to allow *discretion* (nonroutinized action permitting flexible, adaptive, and creative contributions), *recognition* (visibility and notice), and *relevance* (being central to pressing organizational problems).

2. Power also comes when one has relatively close contact with *sponsors* (higher-level people who confer approval, prestige, or backing), *peer networks* (circles of acquaintanceship that provide reputation and information, the grapevine often being faster than formal communication channels), and *subordinates* (who can be developed to relieve managers of some of their burdens and to represent the manager's point of view).

When managers are in powerful situations, it is easier for them to accomplish more. Because the tools are there, they are likely to be highly motivated and, in turn, to be able to motivate subordinates. Their activities are more likely to be on target and to net them successes. They can flexibly interpret or shape policy to meet the needs of particular ar-

2. See my book, *Men and Women of the Corporation* (New York: Basic Books, 1977), pp. 164-205; and David Kipnis, *The Powerholders* (Chicago: University of Chicago Press, 1976).

3. Pehr G Gyllenhammar, *People at Work* (Reading, Mass.: Addison-Wesley, 1977), p. 133.

eas, emergent situations, or sudden environmental shifts. They gain the respect and cooperation that attributed power brings. Subordinates' talents are resources rather than threats. And, because powerful managers have so many lines of connection and thus are oriented outward, they tend to let go of control downward, developing more independently functioning lieutenants.

The powerless live in a different world. Lacking the supplies, information, or support to make things happen easily, they may turn instead to the ultimate weapon of those who lack productive power—oppressive power: holding others back and punishing with whatever threats they can muster.

Exhibit II summarizes some of the major ways in which variables in the organization and in job design contribute to either power or powerlessness.

Positions of powerlessness

Understanding what it takes to have power and recognizing the classic behavior of the powerless can immediately help managers make sense out of a number of familiar organizational problems that are usually attributed to inadequate people:

> The ineffectiveness of first-line supervisors.

> The petty interest protection and conservatism of staff professionals.

> The crises of leadership at the top.

Instead of blaming the individuals involved in organizational problems, let us look at the positions people occupy. Of course, power or powerlessness in a position may not be all of the problem. Sometimes incapable people *are* at fault and need to be retrained or replaced. (See the ruled insert on page 76 for a discussion of another special case, women.) But where patterns emerge, where the troubles associated with some units persist, organizational power failures could be the reason. Then, as Volvo President Pehr Gyllenhammar concludes, we should treat the powerless not as "villains" causing headaches for everyone else but as "victims." [3]

First-line supervisors

Because an employee's most important work relationship is with his or her supervisor, when many

Exhibit I
Some common symbols of a manager's organizational power (influence upward and outward)

To what extent a manager can—

Intercede favorably on behalf of someone in trouble with the organization

Get a desirable placement for a talented subordinate

Get approval for expenditures beyond the budget

Get above-average salary increases for subordinates

Get items on the agenda at policy meetings

Get fast access to top decision makers

Get regular, frequent access to top decision makers

Get early information about decisions and policy shifts

Exhibit II
Ways organizational factors contribute to power or powerlessness

Factors	Generates **power** when factor is	Generates **powerlessness** when factor is
Rules inherent in the job	few	many
Predecessors in the job	few	many
Established routines	few	many
Task variety	high	low
Rewards for reliability/predictability	few	many
Rewards for unusual performance/innovation	many	few
Flexibility around use of people	high	low
Approvals needed for nonroutine decisions	few	many
Physical location	central	distant
Publicity about job activities	high	low
Relation of tasks to current problem areas	central	peripheral
Focus of tasks	outside work unit	inside work unit
Interpersonal contact in the job	high	low
Contact with senior officials	high	low
Participation in programs, conferences, meetings	high	low
Participation in problem-solving task forces	high	low
Advancement prospects of subordinates	high	low

of them talk about "the company," they mean their immediate boss. Thus a supervisor's behavior is an important determinant of the average employee's relationship to work and is in itself a critical link in the production chain.

Yet I know of no U.S. corporate management entirely satisfied with the performance of its supervisors. Most see them as supervising too closely and not training their people. In one manufacturing company where direct laborers were asked on a survey how they learned their job, on a list of seven possibilities "from my supervisor" ranked next to last. (Only company training programs ranked worse.) Also, it is said that supervisors do not translate company policies into practice—for instance, that they do not carry out the right of every employee to frequent performance reviews or to career counseling.

In court cases charging race or sex discrimination, first-line supervisors are frequently cited as the "discriminating official." [4] And, in studies of innovative work redesign and quality of work life projects, they often appear as the implied villains; they are the ones who are said to undermine the program or interfere with its effectiveness. In short, they are often seen as "not sufficiently managerial."

The problem affects white-collar as well as blue-collar supervisors. In one large government agency, supervisors in field offices were seen as the source of problems concerning morale and the flow of information to and from headquarters. "Their attitudes are negative," said a senior official. "They turn people against the agency; they put down senior management. They build themselves up by always complaining about headquarters, but prevent their staff from getting any information directly. We can't afford to have such attitudes communicated to field staff."

Is the problem that supervisors need more management training programs or that incompetent people are invariably attracted to the job? Neither explanation suffices. A large part of the problem lies in the position itself—one that almost universally creates powerlessness.

First-line supervisors are "people in the middle," and that has been seen as the source of many of their problems.[5] But by recognizing that first-line supervisors are caught between higher management and workers, we only begin to skim the surface of the problem. There is practically no other organizational category as subject to powerlessness.

First, these supervisors may be at a virtual dead end in their careers. Even in companies where the job used to be a stepping stone to higher-level management jobs, it is now common practice to bring in MBAs from the outside for those positions. Thus moving from the ranks of direct labor into supervision may mean, essentially, getting "stuck" rather than moving upward. Because employees do not perceive supervisors as eventually joining the leadership circles of the organization, they may see them

as lacking the high-level contacts needed to have clout. Indeed, sometimes turnover among supervisors is so high that workers feel they can outwait—and outwit—any boss.

Second, although they lack clout, with little in the way of support from above, supervisors are forced to administer programs or explain policies that they have no hand in shaping. In one company, as part of a new personnel program supervisors were required to conduct counseling interviews with employees. But supervisors were not trained to do this and were given no incentives to get involved. Counseling was just another obligation. Then managers suddenly encouraged the workers to bypass their supervisors or to put pressure on them. The personnel staff brought them together and told them to demand such interviews as a basic right. If supervisors had not felt powerless before, they did after that squeeze from below, engineered from above.

The people they supervise can also make life hard for them in numerous ways. This often happens when a supervisor has himself or herself risen up from the ranks. Peers that have not made it are resentful or derisive of their former colleague, whom they now see as trying to lord it over them. Often it is easy for workers to break rules and let a lot of things slip.

Yet first-line supervisors are frequently judged according to rules and regulations while being limited by other regulations in what disciplinary actions they can take. They often lack the resources to influence or reward people; after all, workers are guaranteed their pay and benefits by someone other than their supervisors. Supervisors cannot easily control events; rather, they must react to them.

In one factory, for instance, supervisors complained that performance of their job was out of their control: they could fill production quotas only if they had the supplies, but they had no way to influence the people controlling supplies.

The lack of support for many first-line managers, particularly in large organizations, was made dramatically clear in another company. When asked if contact with executives higher in the organization who had the potential for offering support, information, and alliances diminished their own feelings of career vulnerability and the number of headaches they experienced on the job, supervisors in five out of seven work units responded positively. For them

4. William E. Fulmer, "Supervisory Selection: The Acid Test of Affirmative Action," *Personnel*, November-December 1976, p. 40.

5. See my chapter (coauthor, Barry A. Stein), "Life in the Middle: Getting In, Getting Up, and Getting Along," in *Life in Organizations*, eds. Rosabeth M. Kanter and Barry A. Stein (New York: Basic Books, 1979).

Women managers experience special power failures

The traditional problems of women in management are illustrative of how formal and informal practices can combine to engender powerlessness. Historically, women in management have found their opportunities in more routine, low-profile jobs. In staff positions, where they serve in support capacities to line managers but have no line responsibilities of their own, or in supervisory jobs managing "stuck" subordinates, they are not in a position either to take the kinds of risks that build credibility or to develop their own team by pushing bright subordinates.

Such jobs, which have few favors to trade, tend to keep women out of the mainstream of the organization. This lack of clout, coupled with the greater difficulty anyone who is "different" has in getting into the information and support networks, has meant that merely by organizational situation women in management have been more likely than men to be rendered structurally powerless. This is one reason those women who have achieved power have often had family connections that put them in the mainstream of the organization's social circles.

A disproportionate number of women managers are found among first-line supervisors or staff professionals; and they, like men in those circumstances, are likely to be organizationally powerless. But the behavior of other managers can contribute to the powerlessness of women in management in a number of less obvious ways.

One way other managers can make a woman powerless is by patronizingly overprotecting her: putting her in "a safe job," not giving her enough to do to prove herself, and not suggesting her for high-risk, visible assignments. This protectiveness is sometimes born of "good" intentions to give her every chance to succeed (why stack the deck against her?). Out of managerial concerns, out of awareness that a woman may be up against situations that men simply do not have to face, some very well-meaning managers protect their female managers ("It's a jungle, so why send her into it?").

Overprotectiveness can also mask a manager's fear of association with a woman should she fail. One senior bank official at a level below vice president told me about his concerns with respect to a high-performing, financially experienced woman reporting to him. Despite *his* overwhelmingly positive work experiences with her, he was still afraid to recommend her for other assignments because he felt it was a personal risk. "What if other managers are not as accepting of women as I am?" he asked. "I know I'd be sticking my neck out; they would take her more because of my endorsement than her qualifications. And what if she doesn't make it? My judgment will be on the line."

Overprotection is relatively benign compared with rendering a person powerless by providing obvious signs of lack of managerial support. For example, allowing someone supposedly in authority to be bypassed easily means that no one else has to take him or her seriously. If a woman's immediate supervisor or other managers listen willingly to criticism of her and show they are concerned every time a negative comment comes up and that they assume she must be at fault, then they are helping to undercut her. If managers let other people know that they have concerns about this person or that they are testing her to see how she does, then they are inviting other people to look for signs of inadequacy or failure.

Furthermore, people assume they can afford to bypass women because they "must be uninformed" or "don't know the ropes." Even though women may be respected for their competence or expertise, they are not necessarily seen as being informed beyond the technical requirements of the job. There may be a grain of historical truth in this. Many women come to senior management positions as "outsiders" rather than up through the usual channels.

Also, because until very recently men have not felt comfortable seeing women as businesspeople (business clubs have traditionally excluded women), they have tended to seek each other out for informal socializing. Anyone, male or female, seen as organizationally naive and lacking sources of "inside dope" will find his or her own lines of information limited.

Finally, even when women are able to achieve some power on their own, they have not necessarily been able to translate such personal credibility into an organizational power base. To create a network of supporters out of individual clout requires that a person pass on and share power, that subordinates and peers be empowered by virtue of their connection with that person. Traditionally, neither men nor women have seen women as capable of sponsoring others, even though they may be capable of achieving and succeeding on their own. Women have been viewed as the *recipients* of sponsorship rather than as the sponsors themselves.

(As more women prove themselves in organizations and think more self-consciously about bringing along young people,

this situation may change. However, I still hear many more questions from women managers about how they can benefit from mentors, sponsors, or peer networks than about how they themselves can start to pass on favors and make use of their own resources to benefit others.)

Viewing managers in terms of power and powerlessness helps explain two familiar stereotypes about women and leadership in organizations: that no one wants a woman boss (although studies show that anyone who has ever had a woman boss is likely to have had a positive experience), and that the reason no one wants a woman boss is that women are "too controlling, rules-minded, and petty."

The first stereotype simply makes clear that power is important to leadership. Underneath the preference for men is the assumption that, given the current distribution of people in organizational leadership positions, men are more likely than women to be in positions to achieve power and, therefore, to share their power with others. Similarly, the "bossy woman boss" stereotype is a perfect picture of powerlessness. All of those traits are just as characteristic of men who are powerless, but women are slightly more likely, because of circumstances I have mentioned, to find themselves powerless than are men. Women with power in the organization are just as effective — and preferred — as men.

Recent interviews conducted with about 600 bank managers show that, when a woman exhibits the petty traits of powerlessness, people assume that she does so "because she is a woman." A striking difference is that, when a man engages in the same behavior, people assume the behavior is a matter of his own individual style and characteristics and do not conclude that it reflects on the suitability of men for management.

contact was indeed related to a greater feeling of acceptance at work and membership in the organization.

But in the two other work units where there was greater contact, people perceived more, not less, career vulnerability. Further investigation showed that supervisors in these business units got attention only when they were in trouble. Otherwise, no one bothered to talk to them. To these particular supervisors, hearing from a higher-level manager was a sign not of recognition or potential support but of danger.

It is not surprising, then, that supervisors frequently manifest symptoms of powerlessness: overly close supervision, rules-mindedness, and a tendency to do the job themselves rather than to train their people (since job skills may be one of the few remaining things they feel good about). Perhaps this is why they sometimes stand as roadblocks between their subordinates and the higher reaches of the company.

Staff professionals

Also working under conditions that can lead to organizational powerlessness are the staff specialists. As advisers behind the scenes, staff people must sell their programs and bargain for resources, but unless they get themselves entrenched in organizational power networks, they have little in the way of favors to exchange. They are seen as useful adjuncts to the primary tasks of the organization but inessential in a day-to-day operating sense. This disenfranchisement occurs particularly when staff jobs consist of easily routinized administrative functions which are out of the mainstream of the currently relevant areas and involve little innovative decision making.

Furthermore, in some organizations, unless they have had previous line experience, staff people tend to be limited in the number of jobs into which they can move. Specialists' ladders are often very short, and professionals are just as likely to get "stuck" in such jobs as people are in less prestigious clerical or factory positions.

Staff people, unlike those who are being groomed for important line positions, may be hired because of a special expertise or particular background. But management rarely pays any attention to developing them into more general organizational resources. Lacking growth prospects themselves and working alone or in very small teams, they are not in a position to develop others or pass on power to them.

They miss out on an important way that power can be accumulated.

Sometimes staff specialists, such as house counsel or organization development people, find their work being farmed out to consultants. Management considers them fine for the routine work, but the minute the activities involve risk or something problematic, they bring in outside experts. This treatment says something not only about their expertise but also about the status of their function. Since the company can always hire talent on a temporary basis, it is unclear that the management really needs to have or considers important its own staff for these functions.

And, because staff professionals are often seen as adjuncts to primary tasks, their effectiveness and therefore their contribution to the organization are often hard to measure. Thus visibility and recognition, as well as risk taking and relevance, may be denied to people in staff jobs.

Staff people tend to act out their powerlessness by becoming turf-minded. They create islands within the organization. They set themselves up as the only ones who can control professional standards and judge their own work. They create sometimes false distinctions between themselves as experts (no one else could possibly do what they do) and lay people, and this continues to keep them out of the mainstream.

One form such distinctions take is a combination of disdain when line managers attempt to act in areas the professionals think are their preserve and of subtle refusal to support the managers' efforts. Or staff groups battle with each other for control of new "problem areas," with the result that no one really handles the issue at all. To cope with their essential powerlessness, staff groups may try to elevate their own status and draw boundaries between themselves and others.

When staff jobs are treated as final resting places for people who have reached their level of competence in the organization—a good shelf on which to dump managers who are too old to go anywhere but too young to retire—then staff groups can also become pockets of conservatism, resistant to change. Their own exclusion from the risk-taking action may make them resist *anyone's* innovative proposals. In the past, personnel departments, for example, have sometimes been the last in their organization to know about innovations in human

6. Warren Bennis, *The Unconscious Conspiracy: Why Leaders Can't Lead* (New York: AMACOM, 1976).

7. See my chapter, "How the Top is Different," in *Life in Organizations*.

resource development or to be interested in applying them.

Top executives

Despite the great resources and responsibilities concentrated at the top of an organization, leaders can be powerless for reasons that are not very different from those that affect staff and supervisors: lack of supplies, information, and support.

We have faith in leaders because of their ability to make things happen in the larger world, to create possibilities for everyone else, and to attract resources to the organization. These are their supplies. But influence outward—the source of much credibility downward—can diminish as environments change, setting terms and conditions out of the control of the leaders. Regardless of top management's grand plans for the organization, the environment presses. At the very least, things going on outside the organization can deflect a leader's attention and drain energy. And, more detrimental, decisions made elsewhere can have severe consequences for the organization and affect top management's sense of power and thus its operating style inside.

In the go-go years of the mid-1960s, for example, nearly every corporation officer or university president could look—and therefore feel—successful. Visible success gave leaders a great deal of credibility inside the organization, which in turn gave them the power to put new things in motion.

In the past few years, the environment has been strikingly different and the capacity of many organization leaders to do anything about it has been severely limited. New "players" have flexed their power muscles: the Arab oil bloc, government regulators, and congressional investigating committees. And managing economic decline is quite different from managing growth. It is no accident that when top leaders personally feel out of control, the control function in corporations grows.

As powerlessness in lower levels of organizations can manifest itself in overly routinized jobs where performance measures are oriented to rules and absence of change, so it can at upper levels as well. Routine work often drives out nonroutine work. Accomplishment becomes a question of nailing down details. Short-term results provide immediate gratifications and satisfy stockholders or other constituencies with limited interests.

It takes a powerful leader to be willing to risk short-term deprivations in order to bring about desired long-term outcomes. Much as first-line supervisors are tempted to focus on daily adherence to rules, leaders are tempted to focus on short-term fluctuations and lose sight of long-term objectives. The dynamics of such a situation are self-reinforcing. The more the long-term goals go unattended, the more a leader feels powerless and the greater the scramble to prove that he or she is in control of daily events at least. The more he is involved in the organization as a short-term Mr. Fix-it, the more out of control of long-term objectives he is, and the more ultimately powerless he is likely to be.

Credibility for top executives often comes from doing the extraordinary: exercising discretion, creating, inventing, planning, and acting in nonroutine ways. But since routine problems look easier and more manageable, require less change and consent on the part of anyone else, and lend themselves to instant solutions that can make any leader look good temporarily, leaders may avoid the risky by taking over what their subordinates should be doing. Ultimately, a leader may succeed in getting all the trivial problems dumped on his or her desk. This can establish expectations even for leaders attempting more challenging tasks. When Warren Bennis was president of the University of Cincinnati, a professor called him when the heat was down in a classroom. In writing about this incident, Bennis commented, "I suppose he expected me to grab a wrench and fix it." [6]

People at the top need to insulate themselves from the routine operations of the organization in order to develop and exercise power. But this very insulation can lead to another source of powerlessness—lack of information. In one multinational corporation, top executives who are sealed off in a large, distant office, flattered and virtually babied by aides, are frustrated by their distance from the real action. [7]

At the top, the concern for secrecy and privacy is mixed with real loneliness. In one bank, organization members were so accustomed to never seeing the top leaders that when a new senior vice president went to the branch offices to look around, they had suspicion, even fear, about his intentions.

Thus leaders who are cut out of an organization's information networks understand neither what is really going on at lower levels nor that their own isolation may be having negative effects. All too often top executives design "beneficial" new employee programs or declare a new humanitarian policy (e.g., "Participatory management is now our style") only to find the policy ignored or mistrusted because it is perceived as coming from uncaring bosses.

The information gap has more serious consequences when executives are so insulated from the rest of the organization or from other decision makers that, as Nixon so dramatically did, they fail to see their own impending downfall. Such insulation is partly a matter of organizational position and, in some cases, of executive style.

For example, leaders may create closed inner circles consisting of "doppelgängers," people just like themselves, who are their principal sources of organizational information and tell them only what they want to know. The reasons for the distortions are varied: key aides want to relieve the leader of burdens, they think just like the leader, they want to protect their own positions of power, or the familiar "kill the messenger" syndrome makes people close to top executives reluctant to be the bearers of bad news.

Finally, just as supervisors and lower-level managers need their supporters in order to be and feel powerful, so do top executives. But for them sponsorship may not be so much a matter of individual endorsement as an issue of support by larger sources of legitimacy in the society. For top executives the problem is not to fit in among peers; rather, the question is whether the public at large and other organization members perceive a common interest which they see the executives as promoting.

If, however, public sources of support are withdrawn and leaders are open to public attack or if inside constituencies fragment and employees see their interests better aligned with pressure groups than with organizational leadership, then powerlessness begins to set in.

When common purpose is lost, the system's own politics may reduce the capacity of those at the top to act. Just as managing decline seems to create a much more passive and reactive stance than managing growth, so does mediating among conflicting interests. When what is happening outside and inside their organizations is out of their control, many people at the top turn into decline managers and dispute mediators. Neither is a particularly empowering role.

Thus when top executives lose their own lines of supply, lines of information, and lines of support, they too suffer from a kind of powerlessness. The temptation for them then is to pull in every shred of power they can and to decrease the power available to other people to act. Innovation loses out in favor of control. Limits rather than targets are set. Financial goals are met by reducing "overhead" (people) rather than by giving people the tools and discretion to increase their own productive capacity.

Dictatorial statements come down from the top, spreading the mentality of powerlessness farther until the whole organization becomes sluggish and people concentrate on protecting what they have rather than on producing what they can.

When everyone is playing "king of the mountain," guarding his or her turf jealously, then king of the mountain becomes the only game in town.

To expand power, share it

In no case am I saying that people in the three hierarchical levels described are always powerless, but they are susceptible to common conditions that can contribute to powerlessness. *Exhibit III* summarizes the most common symptoms of powerlessness for each level and some typical sources of that behavior.

I am also distinguishing the tremendous concentration of economic and political power in large corporations themselves from the powerlessness that can beset individuals even in the highest positions in such organizations. What grows with organizational position in hierarchical levels is not necessarily the power to accomplish—productive power—but the power to punish, to prevent, to sell off, to reduce, to fire, all without appropriate concern for consequences. It is that kind of power—oppressive power—that we often say corrupts.

The absence of ways to prevent individual and social harm causes the polity to feel it must surround people in power with constraints, regulations, and laws that limit the arbitrary use of their authority. But if oppressive power corrupts, then so does the absence of productive power. In large organizations, powerlessness can be a bigger problem than power.

David C. McClelland makes a similar distinction between oppressive and productive power:

"The negative . . . face of power is characterized by the dominance-submission mode: if I win, you lose. . . . It leads to simple and direct means of feeling powerful [such as being aggressive]. It does not often lead to effective social leadership for the reason that such a person tends to treat other people as pawns. People who feel they are pawns tend to be passive and useless to the leader who gets his sat-

8. David C. McClelland, *Power: The Inner Experience* (New York: Irvington Publishers, 1975), p. 263. Quoted by permission.

Exhibit III
Common symptoms and sources of powerlessness for three key organizational positions

Position	Symptoms	Sources
First-line supervisors	Close, rules-minded supervision	Routine, rules-minded jobs with little control over lines of supply
	Tendency to do things oneself, blocking of subordinates' development and information	Limited lines of information
	Resistant, underproducing subordinates	Limited advancement or involvement prospects for oneself/ subordinates
Staff professionals	Turf protection, information control	Routine tasks seen as peripheral to "real tasks" of line organization
	Retreat into professionalism	Blocked careers
	Conservative resistance to change	Easy replacement by outside experts
Top executives	Focus on internal cutting, short-term results, "punishing"	Uncontrollable lines of supply because of environmental changes
	Dictatorial top-down communications	Limited or blocked lines of information about lower levels of organization
	Retreat to comfort of like-minded lieutenants	Diminished lines of support because of challenges to legitimacy (e.g., from the public or special interest groups)

isfaction from dominating them. Slaves are the most inefficient form of labor ever devised by man. If a leader wants to have far-reaching influence, he must make his followers feel powerful and able to accomplish things on their own. . . . Even the most dictatorial leader does not succeed if he has not instilled in at least some of his followers a sense of power and the strength to pursue the goals he has set." [8]

Organizational power can grow, in part, by being shared. We do not yet know enough about new organizational forms to say whether productive power is infinitely expandable or where we reach the point of diminishing returns. But we do know that sharing power is different from giving or throwing it away. Delegation does not mean abdication.

Some basic lessons could be translated from the field of economics to the realm of organizations and management. Capital investment in plants and equipment is not the only key to productivity. The productive capacity of nations, like organizations, grows if the skill base is upgraded. People with the tools, information, and support to make more informed decisions and act more quickly can often accomplish more. By empowering others, a leader does not decrease his power; instead he may increase it—especially if the whole organization performs better.

This analysis leads to some counterintuitive conclusions. In a certain tautological sense, the principal problem of the powerless is that they lack power. Powerless people are usually the last ones to whom anyone wants to entrust more power, for fear of its dissipation or abuse. But those people are precisely the ones who might benefit most from an injection of power and whose behavior is likely to change as new options open up to them.

Also, if the powerless bosses could be encouraged to share some of the power they do have, their power would grow. Yet, of course, only those leaders who feel secure about their own power outward—their lines of supply, information, and support—can see empowering subordinates as a gain rather than a loss. The two sides of power (getting it and giving it) are closely connected.

There are important lessons here for both subordinates and those who want to change organizations, whether executives or change agents. Instead of resisting or criticizing a powerless boss, which only increases the boss's feeling of powerlessness and need to control, subordinates instead might concentrate on helping the boss become more powerful. Managers might make pockets of ineffectiveness in the organization more productive not by training or replacing individuals but by structural solutions such as opening supply and support lines.

Similarly, organizational change agents who want a new program or policy to succeed should make sure that the change itself does not render any other level of the organization powerless. In making changes, it is wise to make sure that the key people in the level or two directly above and in neighboring functions are sufficiently involved, informed, and taken into account, so that the program can be used to build their own sense of power also. If such involvement is impossible, then it is better to move these people out of the territory altogether than to leave behind a group from whom some power has been removed and who might resist and undercut the program.

In part, of course, spreading power means educating people to this new definition of it. But words alone will not make the difference; managers will need the real experience of a new way of managing.

Here is how the associate director of a large corporate professional department phrased the lessons that he learned in the transition to a team-oriented, participatory, power-sharing management process:

"Get in the habit of involving your own managers in decision making and approvals. But don't abdicate! Tell them what you want and where you're coming from. Don't go for a one-boss grass roots 'democracy.' Make the management hierarchy work for you in participation. . . .

"Hang in there, baby, and don't give up. Try not to 'revert' just because everything seems to go sour on a particular day. Open up—talk to people and tell them how you feel. They'll want to get you back on track and will do things to make that happen—because they don't really want to go back to the way it was. . . . Subordinates will push you to 'act more like a boss,' but their interest is usually more in seeing someone else brought to heel than getting bossed themselves."

Naturally, people need to have power before they can learn to share it. Exhorting managers to change their leadership styles is rarely useful by itself. In one large plant of a major electronics company, first-line production supervisors were the source of numerous complaints from managers who saw them as major roadblocks to overall plant productivity and as insufficiently skilled supervisors. So the plant personnel staff undertook two pilot programs to increase the supervisors' effectiveness. The first program was based on a traditional competency and training model aimed at teaching the specific skills of successful supervisors. The second program, in contrast, was designed to empower the supervisors by directly affecting their flexibility, access to resources, connections with higher-level officials, and control over working conditions.

After an initial gathering of data from supervisors and their subordinates, the personnel staff held meetings where all the supervisors were given tools for developing action plans for sharing the data with their people and collaborating on solutions to perceived problems. But then, in a departure from common practice in this organization, task forces of supervisors were formed to develop new systems for handling job and career issues common to them and their people. These task forces were given budgets, consultants, representation on a plantwide project steering committee alongside managers at much higher levels, and wide latitude in defining the nature and scope of the changes they wished to make. In short, lines of supply, information, and support were opened to them.

As the task forces progressed in their activities, it became clear to the plant management that the hoped-for changes in supervisory effectiveness were taking place much more rapidly through these structural changes in power than through conventional management training; so the conventional training was dropped. Not only did the pilot groups design useful new procedures for the plant, astonishing senior management in several cases with their knowledge and capabilities, but also, significantly, they learned to manage their own people better.

Several groups decided to involve shop-floor workers in their task forces; they could now see from their own experience the benefits of involving subordinates in solving job-related problems. Other supervisors began to experiment with ways to implement "participatory management" by giving subordinates more control and influence without relinquishing their own authority.

Soon the "problem supervisors" in the "most troubled plant in the company" were getting the highest possible performance ratings and were considered models for direct production management. The sharing of organizational power from the top made possible the productive use of power below.

One might wonder why more organizations do not adopt such empowering strategies. There are standard answers: that giving up control is threatening to people who have fought for every shred of it; that people do not want to share power with those they look down on; that managers fear losing their own place and special privileges in the system; that "predictability" often rates higher than "flexibility" as an organizational value; and so forth.

But I would also put skepticism about employee abilities high on the list. Many modern bureaucratic systems are designed to minimize dependence on individual intelligence by making routine as many decisions as possible. So it often comes as a genuine surprise to top executives that people doing the more routine jobs could, indeed, make sophisticated decisions or use resources entrusted to them in intelligent ways.

In the same electronics company just mentioned, at the end of a quarter the pilot supervisory task forces were asked to report results and plans to senior management in order to have their new budget requests approved. The task forces made sure they were well prepared, and the high-level executives were duly impressed. In fact, they were *so* impressed that they kept interrupting the presentations with compliments, remarking that the supervisors could easily be doing sophisticated personnel work.

At first the supervisors were flattered. Such praise from upper management could only be taken well. But when the first glow wore off, several of them became very angry. They saw the excessive praise as patronizing and insulting. "Didn't they think we could think? Didn't they imagine we were capable of doing this kind of work?" one asked. "They must have seen us as just a bunch of animals. No wonder they gave us such limited jobs."

As far as these supervisors were concerned, their abilities had always been there, in latent form perhaps, but still there. They as individuals had not changed—just their organizational power.▽

The redistribution of power

The polarities that I have discussed are those of power and creativity. Workers who want to move in the direction of participative structures will need to confront the issues of power and control. The process of change needs to be mutually shared by all involved, or the outcome will not be a really participative model. The demand for a structural redistribution of power is not sufficient to address the problem of change toward a humanistic, as against a technological, workplace. If we are to change our institutional arrangements from hierarchy to participation, particularly in our workplaces, we will need to look to transformations in ourselves as well. As long as we are imbued with the legitimacy of hierarchical authority, with the sovereignty of the status quo, we will never be able to generate the new and original participative forms that we seek. This means if we are to be equal to the task of reorganizing our workplaces, we need to think about how we can reeducate ourselves and become aware of our own assumptions about the nature of our social life together. Unless the issue is approached in terms of these complexities, I fear that all the worker participation and quality-of-work-life efforts will fail.

From
Robert Schrank, *Ten Thousand Working Days* (Cambridge, MA: The MIT Press, copyright © 1978 by The Massachusetts Institute of Technology). Reprinted with permission of the author.

Reprint 79403

READ THE FINE PRINT

REPRINTS
Telephone: 617-495-6192
Fax: 617-495-6985

Current and past articles are available, as is an annually updated index. Discounts apply to large-quantity purchases.

Please send orders to HBR Reprints Harvard Business School Publishing Division Boston, MA 02163.

HOW CAN *HARVARD BUSINESS REVIEW* ARTICLES WORK FOR YOU?

For years, we've printed a microscopically small notice on the editorial credits page of the *Harvard Business Review* alerting our readers to the availability of *HBR* articles.

Now we invite you to take a closer look at how you can put this hard-working business tool to work for you.

IN THE CORPORATE CLASSROOM

There's no more effective, or cost-effective, way to supplement your corporate training programs than in-depth, incisive *HBR* articles.

At just $3.50 a copy—even less for quantity orders—it's no wonder hundreds of companies use *HBR* articles for management training.

IN-BOX INNOVATION

Where do your company's movers and shakers get their big ideas? Many find inspiration in the pages of *HBR*. They then share the wealth by distributing *HBR* articles to colleagues.

IN MARKETING AND SALES SUPPORT

HBR articles are a substantive leave-behind to your sales calls. They add credibility to your direct mail campaigns. And demonstrate that your company is on the leading edge of business thinking.

CREATE CUSTOM ARTICLES

If you want even greater impact, personalize *HBR* articles with your company's name or logo. And put your name in front of your customers.

DISCOVER MORE REASONS IN THE *HBR CATALOG.*

In all, the *Harvard Business Review Catalog* lists articles on over 500 different subjects. Plus, you'll find collections, books, and videos on subjects you need to know. The catalog is yours for just $10.00. Order today. And start putting *HBR* articles to work for you.

How To Order. To order individual articles or the *HBR Catalog,* dial toll-free in the continental U.S. 1-800-545-7685. Outside the U.S. call 617-495-6192. **Please mention telephone code 165A** when placing your order. Or FAX your order to 617-495-6985. You may also send a check payable to Harvard Business School Publishing Division, or credit card information to: HBR Articles, Harvard Business School Publishing Division, Operations Department, Boston, MA 02163. **All orders must be prepaid.**

Order No.	Title	Qty. X	Price +	Shipping =	Total
21018	Catalog		$10		

U.S. and Canada: 5% for UPS or first class mail. *Foreign Surface Mail:* 15% for parcel post registered; allow 3–6 mos. *Express Deliveries (credit card orders only):* billed at cost; all foreign orders not designating express delivery will be sent by registered surface mail.

☐ Check enclosed (in U.S. funds drawn on U.S. bank)

☐ VISA   ☐ American Express   ☐ MasterCard

Card Number _____ Exp. Date _____

Signature _____

Telephone _____ FAX _____

Name _____

Organization _____

Street _____

City _____

State/Zip _____

Country _____

Harvard Business School Publishing

☐ Home address   ☐ Organization address

PLEASE REFERENCE TELEPHONE ORDER SOURCE CODE 165A

YOU SAID: AND WE SAID:

❝Give us training tools that are relevant to our business...ones we can use *now*.❞

❝We need new cases that stimulate meaningful discussion.❞

❝It can't be a catalog of canned programs... everything we do is custom.❞

❝Make it a single source for up-to-date materials ...on the most current business topics.❞

❝Better yet if it's from a reputable business school. That adds credibility.❞

Harvard Business School Publishing

❝Introducing the Harvard Business School Corporate Training and Development Catalog.❞

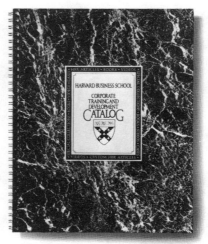

You asked for it. And now it's here.

The new Harvard Business School Corporate Training and Development Catalog is created exclusively for those who design and develop custom training programs.

It's filled cover-to-cover with valuable materials you can put to work on the spot. You'll find a comprehensive selection of cases, *Harvard Business Review* articles, videos, Special Collections, books, and more.

Our new catalog covers the critical management topics affecting corporations today, like Leadership, Quality, Global Business, Marketing, and Strategy, to name a few. And it's all organized, indexed, and cross-referenced to make it easy for you to find precisely what you need.

HOW TO ORDER

To order by FAX, dial 617-495-6985. Or call 617-495-6192. Please mention telephone order code 132A. Or send a check for $10 payable to HBS Publishing Division, or credit card information to: HBS Corporate Training and Development Catalog, Harvard Business School Publishing Division, Operations Department, Boston, MA 02163. **All orders must be prepaid.**

Order No.	Title	Qty. ×	Price +	Shipping* =	Total
39001	Catalog		$10		

*U.S. and Canada: 5% for UPS or first class mail. *Foreign Surface Mail:* 15% for parcel post registered; allow 3–6 mos. *Express Deliveries (credit card orders only):* billed at cost; all foreign orders not designating express delivery will be sent by registered surface mail.

☐ Check enclosed (in U.S. funds drawn on U.S. bank)

☐ VISA   ☐ American Express   ☐ MasterCard

Card Number_____ Exp. Date_____

Signature_____

Telephone_____ FAX_____

Name_____

Organization_____

Street_____

City_____ State/Zip_____

Country_____ ☐ Home Address ☐ Organization Address

Please Reference Telephone Order Source Code 132A